Refusal and Transgression
in
Joyce Carol Oates' Fiction

Refusal and Transgression in Joyce Carol Oates' Fiction

Marilyn C. Wesley

Contributions in Women's Studies, Number 135

GREENWOOD PRESS
Westport, Connecticut • London

Library of Congress Cataloging-in-Publication Data

Wesley, Marilyn C.
    Refusal and transgression in Joyce Carol Oates' fiction / Marilyn
C. Wesley.
        p.   cm.   —   (Contributions in women's studies, ISSN 0147–104X ;
no.   135)
    Includes bibliographical references and index.
    ISBN 0–313–28462–8
    1. Oates, Joyce Carol, 1938–   —Criticism and interpretation.
2. Family in literature. I. Title. II. Series.
PS3565.A8Z96   1993
813'.54—dc20   92–39467

British Library Cataloguing in Publication Data is available.

Library of Congress Catalog Card Number: 92–39467
ISBN: 0–313–28462–8
ISSN: 0147–104X

First published in 1993

Greenwood Press, 88 Post Road West, Westport, CT 06881
An imprint of Greenwood Publishing Group, Inc.

Printed in the United States of America

The paper used in this book complies with the
Permanent Paper Standard issued by the National
Information Standards Organization (Z39.48–1984).

10 9 8 7 6 5 4 3 2

For Norman

Contents

Preface

In March of 1986 Elaine Showalter published an article in *Ms*. magazine entitled "My Friend, Joyce Carol Oates." More than a personal account, the essay also claims Oates as a friend of the feminist movement: "despite the series of important books on female experience she has written especially during this decade, Oates has never had the acknowledgment from feminist readers and critics that she deserves" (44). *Refusal and Transgression* is intended to theorize a basis for the well-deserved feminist appreciation of Oates' valuable oeuvre.

Jonathan Culler hypothesizes several key "moments" in feminist literary criticism. The first assumes that a reader's experience is continuous with a text and, therefore, "takes considerable interest in the situations and psychology of female characters, investigating attitudes to women or the 'images of women' in the works of an author, a genre, or a period" (46). Proceeding from this postulate, much early feminist consideration condemned Oates for presenting disappointing portraits of women. Oates' first critics described her moving portrayal of female victims, the "unliberated women" of Joyce Carol Oates, in Joanne Creighton's influential phrase, without observing her corresponding tactics of liberation. My study makes use of significant changes in the methods and objectives of more recent feminist theory and the theoretical practice of post-structuralism, Marxism, and psychology to discover in Joyce Carol Oates' fiction of the American family systematic strategies of resistance.

In the introduction to a 1983 volume of essays in women's history, Judith Newton, Mary P. Ryan, and Judith R. Walkowitz note an important methodological shift from an "earlier focus on victimization" toward an effort to reconceptualize "the very nature and locus of power" (7). Oates' *oeuvre,* comprised in large measure of the narratives of sons and daughters, is an extended meditation on the institution of the family as the "locus" of the definition and dissemination of social and economic power through the gendered psychological experience of its members. Materialist-feminist criticism, which takes as its focus, according to Judith Newton and Deborah Rosenfelt in their 1987 *Feminist Criticism and Social Change*, "not the tale of individual and inevitable suffering, but a story of struggle and relations of power" (xv), furnishes a basis for an approach to the analysis of the power dynamics of Oates' domestic fiction.

Central to such criticism is the examination of ideology, "a structure of perception that helps maintain a particular set of social and economic relations at a particular juncture in history" (xxii). For otherwise, as Josephine Donovan explained in 1989, "unexamined ideologies . . . function as fate" (xiii). Feminist criticism is able to examine the operation of ideology, according to Gayle Greene and Coppelia Kahn in their 1985 survey of feminist scholarship, through attention to the "partial truths and contradictions that ideology masks" (22). The striking contradictions at the heart of Oates' fiction are registered in the vigorous attempts of her daughters and sons, repeated and refined from work to work in serial gestures of what I am calling *refusal* and *transgression*, to evade or redefine their gendered fates, and in the dialectic struggle of the text itself against the codes that support it through the projection of what I define as Oates' *feminist unconscious* and its narrative agent, the recurrent figure of the *transgressive other*.

Ideology in the Althusserian sense developed in this study refers to the acceptance of a single and restrictive story, one familiar fiction which fails to tell the unknown and multiple stories contained in a vast "unconscious" of possible versions. The limiting story that determines Oates' texts is the patriarchal gender system imposed by the family. But the sub-text of Oates' fiction is to be found in the narrative strategies, which resist and attempt to subvert that system.

In her 1982 preface to *Writing and Sexual Difference*, Elizabeth Abel pointed out that women's writing may mount a challenge from within patriarchal discourse through acts of "revision, appropriation, and subversion" (2). Joyce Carol Oates' domestic fiction—narratives that treat the characters, the relations, and the frequently extreme emotional experiences of the modern family—actively controverts the gender assumptions upon which that family is structured through the revision and appropriation of specific literary forms and through the general patterns of narrative subversion I describe as *refusal* and *transgression*. In so doing, Oates' texts interrogate the social and economic systems of power in which the family participates.

A criticism with this political intent will, in Donovan's view, consider the text as a dialectic between its "negative" subversion of dominant ideology and its "positive" aspiration. Citing Fredric Jameson, Donovan describes the "positive" objective of the feminist critic as identifying the "text's liberatory function" and delineating its "utopian horizon" (xvii). While Oates' works challenge the detrimental operation of gender ideology in the family, they also struggle to "solve" the gendered contradictions they uncover and to redefine the family as a utopian model of social cooperation.

Finally, feminist criticism, as Newton and Rosenfelt characterize it, will subsume to its task the productive insights of many related disciplines, and my literary investigation of the refusals and transgressions of Oates' oeuvre makes use of the diverse scholarship of post-structuralism, Marxism, and psychology, as well as feminism. Although it was certainly initially important to catalogue and excoriate the female victimization so richly implied in women's fiction, it is now necessary to employ and extend a methodology for the analysis of the corollary strategies of active resistance and redefinition in which that fiction is also engaged. In addition to securing for Joyce Carol Oates the feminist recognition her work clearly deserves, this study is intended as a contribution to the development of a contemporary critical practice which can better account for the revolutionary potential of women's fiction.

But Oates' work has been examined from perspectives other than that of feminism. The general problem with that criticism to date, however, is a failure to discern and describe an underlying structure uniting the diverse plots, characters, styles, and genres of her prodigious oeuvre. This book maintains that family, power, and resistance, concepts interacting throughout Oates' fiction, provide the key to understanding the genesis, energy, and meaning of her works. Briefly, the complicated stories of various characters in many different settings typically take place in the context of family relationships, and since the institution of the family directly shapes individual perception of the social and financial forces of the greater world, Oates' disturbing portrayals of troubled families can and do address complex issues of power in contemporary society—economic dislocation, gender inequity, and violence—as they are experienced in intimate relationships. And if plot in Oates' work customarily deals with the family, theme always concerns complicated issues of personal, familial, and public power. Oates' characteristic stance towards the plot of family and the theme of power is challenging, interrogative, even revolutionary resistance.

The patriarchal family of Oates' fiction is more than an arrangement of individuals; it is a system for the allocation and definition of power. The father, whose role as financial provider gives him access to the social sources of power in economic or ideological institutions, has primary responsibility for imposing the power experienced by other family members, and that experience is further regulated by gender. Traditionally, the father's power provides the resources for adequate nurture by the mother, the son grows up to replicate his father's power, and the daughter assumes her mother's complementary supportive function. The difficulty, as Oates' fiction presents it, is that this traditional arrangement is not working. Historical shifts in the larger social and economic world, which are mostly unrecognized in the circumscribed spheres of individual characters, have invalidated the fathers' traditional interpretations of their own power, and as a result of the deficiency of the fathers' power, dependent mothers are usually inadequately nurturant and children constantly struggle against the inappropriate gender expectations fostered by their experience in traditional families. The narratives of this struggle by the sons and daughters of Oates' fiction develop in marked patterns of resistance which I define as refusal and transgression. Through their efforts to refuse the models implied by the lives of same-sex parents and through the even more provocative challenges implied by transgressive relations with parents of the opposite sex, Oates' young protagonists enact a trenchant critique of the American family and of the society which has formed it.

Refusal and Transgression
in
Joyce Carol Oates' Fiction

Introduction: Family, Power, Resistance

Family. Power. Resistance. These terms are the key to understanding the urgency and the effectiveness of Joyce Carol Oates' fiction. At last count, she was the author of twenty-six novels. A recent collection of interviews with the author lists her collected work as eighty-seven volumes (Milazzo v), and the 1986 comprehensive bibliography cites 397 separate short stories (Lercangée 7–45). This vast oeuvre contains an impressive variety of characters with at least one thing in common: the men, women, adolescents, children, rebels, martyrs, members of the professions and the unemployed, would-be saints and definite sinners, the wooden Virgin and the Oriental goddess of love who appear and come to life in her pages are most often presented in the context of family relationship.

Oates' critics frequently insist that her fiction centers on repetitive plots and central obsessions.[1] She herself remarks, "Everything is related. If it wouldn't alarm me, I'd someday go back through all my writing and note how the obsessions come and go horizontally (a single psychological 'plot' worked out in a story, a play, poems, parts of novels)" ("Transformations of Self" 50). That obsessive plot is, I believe, the story of the American family, not its nostalgic resurrection but its painful adjustments to a changing world.

In Oates' fiction we minutely observe the modern family from the period of the Depression to the present in the throes of change. Mediating as it does between the individual and society, the family is affected by historical change slowly but radically. Although the family is the social institution "most resistant to change," according to Christopher Lasch, any alteration in its size, emotional arrangement, or relation to society "must have enormous impact on the development of personality." And "changes in character structure, in turn, accompany or underlie changes in economic and political life" (4). Oates' domestic fiction is concerned with both of these types of change. Especially in her early work, economic changes in the larger world affect families in such a way as to change individuals, but the correlative project throughout has been to define individual resistance to family ideology, which may in turn contribute to the restructuring of the social world.

Characters in Oates' fiction will understand *family* to refer to the traditional standard—breadwinning father, nurturing mother, and siblings of assorted gender—but the reader of Oates' fiction will observe another pattern frequently undermining the first. The father, and perhaps even his father if the family is extended, may be brutal, weak, financially inadequate or absent, whereas the mother or grandmother may provide inadequate or irrelevant care to her children. And as these children approach adulthood they will energetically attempt to evade the roles modeled by their parents' lives. But Oates is not merely depicting dysfunctional families; the dysfunctional relationships she presents serve to question expectations about the operation of family structure.

The concept of power in Oates' work extends from the possibility of global warfare to the opportunity for personal agency,[2] but at whatever level it is examined it is consistently marked by the failure of the father as its agent and the harmful consequences to other family members. Oates' domestic relationships, then, both articulate and challenge contemporary definitions of power mediated through the gender system of the patriarchal family. In brief, if the plot of Oates' fiction centers on the modern family, its theme questions the contemporary meaning of power. As I shall argue, the failure of ideal power relations in Oates' families reveals power and nurturance as the exclusive attributes of father and mother to be an anachronistic social adaptation resulting in a central opposition that produces impotence and isolation as the respective characteristics of daughters and sons. The experience of these restrictions provokes the patterns of resistance I define as refusal and transgression.

Yet Oates' characteristic strategies of resistance have been too often inadequately understood. Her introduction to the 1981 critical collection *Contraries* states that "the seven essays in this volume, written over a period of approximately twenty years . . . were originally stimulated by feelings of opposition, and in one or two cases, a deep and passionate revulsion" (viii). The philosophic basis in creative "opposition" specified here in Oates' criticism has, however, long been a source of confusion in her fiction. In 1979 Linda Wagner surveyed the striking variation in critical response to Oates' works (xxiii–xxiv) and Joanne Creighton noted that readers have often been unable to relate the deterministic expectations invoked by Oates' naturalistic techniques to the "modernistic formulation" of her "visionary conception" (*Joyce Carol Oates* 149, 144). This seeming discrepancy, which marred Oates' accomplishment for Creighton in 1979, may be better understood with reference to Catherine Belsey's 1980 modalities of the "declarative" and "interrogative" text.

Belsey's formulations grow out of post-structuralist and deconstructive literary theory, which, like Oates' work, discovers virtue in contradiction. Using naturalistic description, the declarative text masks its fictivity and tends toward comfortable closure, thereby endorsing the "hierarchy of discourses" of its own culture (92), whereas the interrogative text, in contrast, "disrupts the unity of the reader" (91) by employing the author as a locus of question and contradiction. Oates' fiction employs both practices. Typically declarative in its descriptive evocation of the textures of an actual world, it also unfolds in narrative patterns of resistance and consistently decenters the reader by imposing the discomfort of incomplete closure. Oates' texts also formally question a number of romantic assumptions and a variety of generic practices that reinforce dominant ideology.

Because of this dual perspective, in order to appreciate Joyce Carol Oates' fiction, the reader must heed the dialectic struggle between the text's declarative evocation of what is and its interrogative challenge in the service of what might be. Feminism, through its careful analysis of women's experience and its thoughtful articulation of alternative possibility, can provide the discursive basis for such an encounter. Although Oates rejects the limitation of feminist designation[3] and despite frequent claims that her work has been anti-feminist,[4] to read her family fiction in the post-structural double light of revealing contradiction discloses an *oeuvre* exhaustively engaged in testing the restrictions imposed by gendered power arrangements. And to read Oates' work in this way is to read it as feminist revolution in the making.

POWER AND THE FAMILY

In the title story of Joyce Carol Oates' 1984 collection, the central character remarks "that the family is a vanishing animal in the United States, doomed to extinction" (*Last Days* 22), a comment that exaggerates the preoccupation of Oates' fiction from the outset: the family—not its actual demise but its damaged and diminished effectiveness. Consider the first story in her first collection of stories as an illustration of the declining effectiveness of the family intersected by the issues of power and resistance. In "Swamps," the Grandfather, who inhabits a "log cabin," (*By the North Gate* 13) is a character out of history tinged by legend. It is the Grandfather's responsibility to transmit to his seven-year-old grandson his own positive values: "This-here is a damn good world, a *god*-damn good world, it's all you got an' you better pay attention to it" (17). But the Grandfather's world has failed. The old man's son, forced to abandon farming the unprofitable land for work in the gypsum mill, is "sick of gypsum dust in his lungs, sick of the foreman, sick of working underground, sick of the cheese sandwiches he carried for lunch everyday; he was sick of life" (13).

Between these clashing worldviews wanders a strange young girl, confused, pregnant, and alone. Through the birth of her child traditional values are to be validated, the sanctity of the family is to be reconstituted. The weakening old man assumes responsibility for the expectant mother; by becoming Joseph to her Mary he resumes heroic stature, and on the night of the birth the boy witnesses a resurrection of joy even in his own world-weary father. But in the clear light of the day after this birth and rebirth, the family finds the grandfather bruised and unconscious. The girl has bashed him with a board and run away. The boy discovers the infant drowned in a basin of the sewage-polluted water from the creek that flows beside the old man's junk-strewn cabin. If ever a story demonstrated the contradiction between family ideology and family reality, that story is "Swamps."

In 1911 the traditional functions of the family were described as

the management of the household, the reproduction, rearing and education of children, the control of population growth and of genetic lines, the development of sociableness, the care of the sick and elderly, the accumulation and hereditary transmission of capital and other property, as well as the determination of choice of occupation.[5]

But in "Swamps" the family fails demonstrably at all these functions. Let us briefly consider the points in order.

The boy lives with his mother and father and sister in a traditional and orderly household, as is apparent in the efficiency of the mother's kitchen. But the condition of the shadow household of the nearly senile old man and the crazed girl undercuts this version. The grandfather does not even possess the rudiments necessary for birth, for family continuity: " 'I'm needin' a good clean knife, for one thing,' he said apologetically. . . . 'An' some towels or so...a sheet, maybe. . . . For when she's due' " (21).⁶

The baby's death and the boy's confusion controverts the family's central function in the rearing and education of children. The unknown and husbandless girl denies family control of "population growth" along predictable "genetic lines." The grandfather's attempt to aid the unfortunate girl provides a negative lesson in "sociableness" for the boy. The mother's attempt to care for the Grandfather is kindly but largely ineffectual. The legitimate capital acquisitions of the family have been reduced to uncultivated land and a junk-filled cabin, worthless to the father and the boy who follows him, and certainly the father's example shows that the "choice of occupation" has become an accident of the economy rather than a family prerogative.

What, then, does the family do? The answer lies in the one birthright with which the Grandfather may endow the boy—an orientation toward authority. The mother respects the old man's "prickly independence. 'You must be like your grandfather,' she would whisper to the little boy. 'When you grow up. Not now, but when you grow up' " (12).

Independence and its opposite term *submission* are, according to Max Horkheimer, both useful responses to authority. The sources of these contradictory responses are varying economic conditions of a society mediated through its institutions, especially the family:

The growing child experiences the influence of reality according as the latter is reflected in the mirror of the family circle. The family, as one of the most formative agencies, sees to it that the kind of human character emerges which social life requires and gives this human being in great measure the indispensible adaptability for a specific authority-oriented conduct on which the existence [of his own social order] depends. (98)

This education in authority-orientation occurs in Western society as a seemingly natural consequence of the patriarchal structure of the family: "with its two-fold foundation in the father's economic position and his physical strength with its legal backing" (107). "Swamps," however, is a story of patriarchy that splits, and thereby qualifies, Horkheimer's archetypal father as a source of unproblematic adaptation to authority. The power of the boy's father rests on his financial support of the family, and it is evident that the family's economic survival in this story depends on his ability to submit to the regimentation of the factory. Indeed, the father's depression is at least partly a result of the confusing and inappropriate orientation he received from his own father, who still retains remnants of the legal and physical strength that supported an independence appropriate to the Grandfather's pioneer background. As a result of these divergent patriarchal models, the boy's inadequate alternatives vacillate between stifling submission and ineffectual independence.

From the beginning, Oates' fiction presents in the often split figure of the father the concept of power undergoing economically determined change. The dislocation from the smallholding to the factory has resulted in a crisis in traditional definitions. As this story illustrates, the concept of power in Oates' works is the product of complex mediation. And although it is derived primarily from the father's problematic adaptation to poorly understood economic authority, it is further complicated by insertion into gender ideology.

As an instance of ideological complexity, the boy must not only make sense of the two different modes of his father and Grandfather, but he must try, as well, to resolve two grandfathers, the mythic and the actual. The first emerges during visits with Old Hamp. The two aged cronies share afternoons of fishing, drinking, and leisurely reminiscence that always culminate in their clumsy attempts to shave one another with an old straight razor, "grinning with blood running in glistening streams down their faces" (15). At these moments, the Grandfather embodies pure, primitive patriarchal power: " 'You, there, boy!' he would yell drunkenly, 'You want me to cut out your gizzard for you?' " (16). Yet the boy is unable to reconcile this primal figure with the "trembling old man who whined about being robbed" (27) at the end of the story. This emphasis on the boy's bewilderment indicates that Oates' focus is not the realistic analysis of economic forces that have dislocated the concept of power, which her works characteristically relegate to symbolic setting—the cabin and the gypsum mill of this story, the Eden County, Detroit, or Fernwood of her novels. Rather, her concern is with the effect of that dislocation.

The problem of gender ideology is demonstrated by the reactions of the young man and the young woman of the story. The stock figure of the boy registers the confusing reorientation to authority in the traditional family, whereas the violent resistance of the innovative character, the pregnant girl, reflects the extent to which this reorientation may challenge the structure of the family. When the Grandfather and the boy find her at the creek bank, she has been swearing at school children, throwing bits of dried mud to frighten them away: "You an' them goddam kids go away and let me be. I got a right to sit here all I want" (18). The girl's cantankerous independence forges an immediate bond with the Grandfather, so he attempts to solve the problems of each of them traditionally, by taking the girl into his home and assuming paternal responsibility for her delivery.

Horkheimer suggests two roles for a woman. She may provide maternal love, and she may strengthen the man's orientation to authority by "chaining" him to "the status quo" (118, 120). The nurturant mother in the story enacts the first role, whereas the sister, whom the Grandfather reproaches for a conventionality that precludes humane concern, performs the second. But the defiant girl rejects both traditional feminine definitions. She luridly refuses the maternal role, and she violently transgresses the patriarchal status quo represented by the legitimation inherent in the proffered protection of the Grandfather.

At its inception "Swamps" shadows forth characteristic concerns that Joyce Carol Oates will develop and refine throughout her career: the focus on a point of change, the exploration of modes and definitions of power, the inquiry into the meaning of gender, the concentration on the family as it is constituted by and constitutes social experience, and the revolutionary challenge evident in complex patterns of refusal and transgression, which it is my purpose here to set forth.

In contrast to Horkheimer's theory of adaptive masculine alternatives, the ideology of gender operating in Oates' fiction prescribes independence as appropriate orientation to authority for the male and submission for the female, but the changing social and economic conditions in "Swamps" effect a challenge to this rigid formula. The boy must question his assignment, whereas the girl subverts hers. In Hemingway's "Big Two-Hearted River," the hero can choose to fish the swamp on another day; Oates' family must find new ways to live within it.

RESISTANCE AND THE FAMILY

The work of Fredric Jameson provides a convenient means of conceptualizing Oates' varied presentations of family relations as interrogation of traditional ideology. According to Jameson, all forms of power and status are "based ultimately on gender hierarchy and on the building block of the family unit," a conjoined base providing the "juncture" between Marxism and feminism: "the moment at which the feminist project and the Marxist and socialist project meet and face the same dilemma: how to imagine Utopia" ("Cognitive Mapping" 355). To consider the institution of the family, therefore, is to raise issues of both class and gender. And in such a consideration, the methods of Jameson's literary interpretation of class relations may be productively applied to feminist analysis of gender relations.

Imagining Utopia is, in Jameson's opinion, precisely what narrative is struggling to accomplish, but the novel must attempt to resolve in fiction the actual problems resulting from its location within a particular society. And as a form of ideology—in which real conditions are obscured by imaginary circumstances[7]—narrative can neither directly portray the problem that motivates it nor produce the real situation necessary to its utopian solution. To conceive of literature in Jamesonian terms is to understand it as a system characterized by the "restless energy" of "its desperate attempt to square its own circles and to produce new terms out of itself which ultimately 'solve' the dilemma at hand" (*The Political Unconscious* 254). To read Joyce Carol Oates' literature in this way is to trace resistance as a structural imperative, a response to the ideological limits that shape it, and to comprehend the energy of her literary production as reflective of the intensity of the problem of family, gender, and power it addresses.

For Jameson, then, fiction inscribes its struggles against limitations imposed by social circumstance. He adapts to its interpretation A. J. Greimas' model of the elementary structure of signification to uncover the terms of that struggle.[8] Greimas' structural prototype, which purports to schematize the fundamental mental processes that organize reality through the negation of two terms of an initial logical opposition, is reinterpreted by Jameson to articulate the systematic operation of narrative encountering an insoluble social antinomy. In this situation, according to Jameson, the text attempts to resolve the original contradiction by working its way through the narrative possibilities generated by the initial terms according to the trajectory charted by Greimas' "semiotic rectangle." In Greimas' system an originary term S generates an opposing term $-S$, which exists in a relation of logical contradiction. Each of these terms generates terms of negation: not S and not $-S$ in the following diagram:

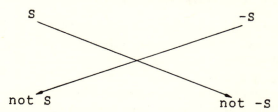

Greimas and François Rastier exemplify the operation of this system through the explication of the "social model of sexual relations" (93–98). Following their lead Jameson has adapted the structuralist model to broader social inquiry by substituting for the logical opposition of the primary terms a relation of social contradiction. In Oates' fiction such a social contradiction exists between the terms *Power* and *Nurturance* and the negations of these primary terms produce the following relational permutations:

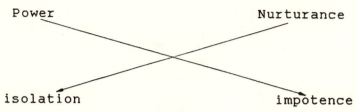

Because Jameson's application of Greimas is both economically presented and conceptually complex, it is useful here to illustrate the theory with reference to the family relationships of "Swamps." As we have observed, the ideology of family cooperation—the ideal union of the powerful father and the nurturant mother that supports the family and encourages replication of its structure—is disputed by the action of the story. In fact, a general consideration of Oates' fiction reveals that instead of cooperative union, power and nurturance, personified by the father and mother, operate in an ineffectual relationship of disjuncture that this story merely implies. The crucial knowledge, which Jameson's adaptation of Greimas makes available, is that such a disjuncture has further consequences: in fiction, which discloses the effects of conflict, each of the original terms produces a negation. As I see it, in Oates' work the negation of *power* is *impotence* and the negation of *nurturance* is the inability to connect with others in an intimate relation, which I have termed *isolation*. Since the disjuncture of power and nurturance is defined as family structure and experienced as family relationship, the secondary terms may also be personified by family members. Just as the father is allied with power, his negation, the family member who is supposed to be most unlike him—the daughter—embodies powerlessness. Similarly, the son, most unlike the mother, is defined by isolation, the negation of nurturance. In these relationships we may observe the basic conditions of the gender ideology shaping the traditional family, and it is a pattern we will recognize from Freudian theory.

According to Freud, when the young boy reaches his oedipal crisis he must relinquish his close attachment to his mother in order to assume the privileged power of his father's situation. "Swamps" indicates this necessity through the boy's thematic immersion in the complex issues of power. Oates' works, in which the teenage son has already reached the stage of oedipal transition, highlight his angry and confused exclusion in addition to his questions about power. Excluded from maternal attachment, he is, consequently, "isolated."

In Freudian psychology the crucial moment for the young woman is her realization that she does not possess the phallus, that organic symbol of masculine power. The physical reality of the woman is thought to represent her inevitable "impotence," her painful exclusion from the father's power. It is therefore her endeavor to assume an appropriate role of nurturance in order to secure a permanent bond with a partner, a man who possesses the power of the phallus and can make good her shattering loss. Her nurturant propensity also encourages her to have a child, which Freud theorizes as another means of replacing the absent phallus.

We see these basic terms of the Freudian equation both presented and subverted in "Swamps." In addition to sketching the ideological structure, as we have seen, the story also works to displace it. The unfortunate girl in the story, for example, is definitely powerless, but her actions and relationships clearly resist the Freudian predication of a nurturant role as a means of reparation: the drowned infant graphically signifies this rejection. We may plot both the story's ideological structure and its systematic subversion in figure 1. The solid square in the center represents the family system, whereas the broken lines forming the exterior rectangle display the subversions of role expectation the story generates. The solid line between the girl and the mother, for example, suggests that the girl should replicate the maternal role, but the broken line of the rectangle plots the girl's shocking refusal. Similarly, the boy's expected identification with the paternal role, indicated by the solid line, is thwarted in the narrative development of the story; the broken line of the rectangle represents an alternative narrative position of "confusion."

This schematic analysis of the first story can serve to reveal, as well, the structure underlying the totality of Joyce Carol Oates' family fiction. Just as identification between grandson and father figure, pregnant girl and mother, are resisted in "Swamps," all the dyadic relations in Oates' families repeatedly demonstrate similar marked patterns of resistance. In a wide range of plots and settings, mother-daughter, father-son, and brother-sister relationships consistently produce the narrative patterns I define as *refusal*, and the connections between mothers and sons and fathers and daughters, like the unsettling alliance of the girl and the Grandfather here, result in the provocative narratives I describe as *transgression*. Thus, the object of this analysis of "Swamps"—the articulation of both the terms of the restrictive ideological system of family relationship and the narrative patterns that register resistance to this system—may be extended to an overview of all of Oates' family fiction.

In the comprehensive representation of Oates' oeuvre the basic Greimasian structure operates as it does in Jameson's analysis of *Nostromo*

Figure 1

"Swamps"

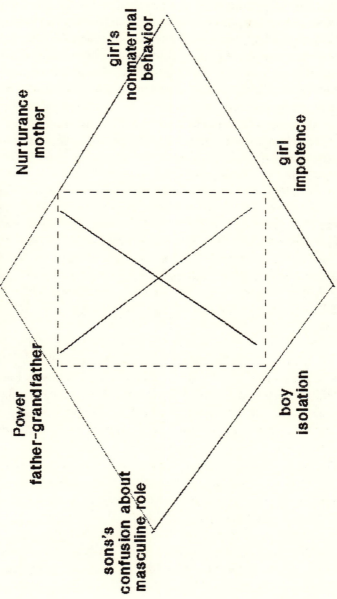

- failure to establish patriarchal family of girl and the Grandfather
- Nurturance mother
- girl's nonmaternal behavior
- girl impotence
- no relationship
- boy isolation
- sons's confusion about masculine role
- Power father-grandfather

in *The Political Unconscious* (254), so that specific works supply characters for the ideological positions created by the social contradiction and predict relationships between these characters. However, instead of fulfilling the ideological expectations of the family system, the actual relationships between family members introduce a range of alternatives to the misalliance of power and nurturance, the initiating problem that Oates' fiction is attempting to solve. As in the schematic model of "Swamps," the central square schematizes the ideology of gender as it is experienced in the Oates family, whereas the character relations growing out of this base structure represent narrative struggles to resist its imposition. A full articulation of the implications of character relations in Joyce Carol Oates' family fiction is represented in figure 2.

The chapters that follow interpret the elements of this model. Chapter 1 considers the decline of Father to father and Mother to mother as this "fall" is presented in Oates' early works. *With Shuddering Fall* and *A Garden of Earthly Delights*, Oates' first two novels, and *Upon the Sweeping Flood*, her first collection of short stories, invoke the ideal of the all-powerful Mother and Father only to record the demotion of these god-like figures into the fallen state of ordinary and flawed parents whose failure of cooperative power and nurturance is the problem motivating Oates' fiction.

Moving in a clockwise direction about the diagram, Chapter 2 charts the relationship of mothers and daughters as the first instance of the striking pattern of refusal that this schematic analysis makes apparent. In addition to proposing a developmental model of the daughters' maturation, the second chapter argues that the daughters are not the passive victims so often described in previous commentary on Oates' work; instead, the relationships between mother and daughter in *them* and *Childwold* demonstrate the daughters' active unwillingness to simply accept their mothers' unexamined powerlessness. The daughters confront feminine impotence and attempt to avoid, correct, or control it, and this conscious effort defines what I call their "Refusal of Innocence."

Chapter 3 considers the relation of brother and sister in the position at the bottom of the diagram that I label "Refusal of Substitute Weak Family Unit." For example, *them* and *Angel of Light*, despite portrayals of genuine family bonds, end with the separation of siblings. Since the bottom set of terms results from negations, a union between impotent sister and isolate brother would imply failure to confront limitation. Although all of Oates' works explore relations of power, and most concern a daughter or a son or both as central characters, none endorses the union of sister and brother

Figure 2
The Semiotic Structure of Joyce Carol Oates' Family Fiction

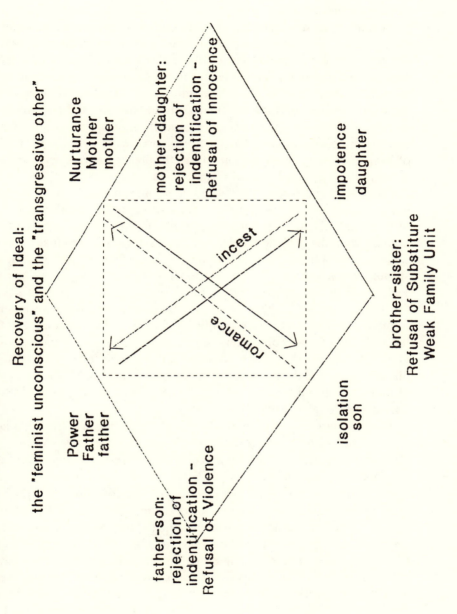

Recovery of Ideal:
the "feminist unconscious" and the "transgressive other"

Nurturance
Mother
mother

mother-daughter:
rejection of
indentification –
Refusal of Innocence

impotence
daughter

brother-sister:
Refusal of Substiture
Weak Family Unit

isolation
son

Power
Father
father

father-son:
rejection of
indentification –
Refusal of Violence

incest

romance

as a unit of resolution for problems posed by the gendered negations of power and nurturance.

Chapter 4, entitled the "Refusal of Violence" treats a major focus in Oates' fiction: the evolution of the sons' refusal to identify themselves with the practice of power defined by the fathers. In *A Garden of Earthly Delights* the problem of power results in the son's murder of the father. In *them*, too, the son murders a symbolic father. These acts of violence indicate rejection of fathers, but by employing the fathers' mode of authority—violence—the sons paradoxically indicate an acceptance of interpretations of authority that destroy themselves as well. It is the project of *Wonderland*, in which the son refuses the prerogatives of serial fathers, to suggest Oates' resolution of this dilemma.

Chapters 5 and 6 refer to the middle section of the diagram, which I identify as the axis of transgression. Not a feature of Jameson's application of Greimas, this analysis may be appended to that model. In this axis of transgression the directional arrow indicates a reversal originating in the weak terms with the object of destroying the negations imposed by the strong. In transgressive relationships with opposite-sex parents the son seeks to evade his position of isolation through stylized ritual courtship of the mother, and the daughter seeks to reverse her perceived powerlessness through a connection with a symbolic father. The broken line indicates that the schemes of reappropriation—figuratively called *incest* and *romantic love*—fail: daughter and son do not secure for themselves the power or nurturance denied them as a result of oedipal alignment, but the narratives of these transgressive patterns uncover the defects of the gender ideology operating through the traditional family.

The romantic love considered in Chapter Five has as object a lost or inaccessible woman addressed through chivalric gestures. Mother-son relationships of this kind appear in *Expensive People* and *Wonderland*, and the mode is extended to a boy-girl relation in *them*. Involved in this transgressive maneuver, the son avoids the issue of power, a regression often presented in a tone bordering on derision. But although the romantic transgressions of mother and son are touched by ridicule, the extensive treatment of the daughter-father transgression—the subject of Chapter 6—is very serious indeed. The dream of this relationship informs *With Shuddering Fall*. The inclusion of a serious short story on this theme almost destroys the humorous impact of *Expensive People*. Important in *Do with Me What You Will*, it is fully explored in *Childwold*. It is re-articulated in *Angel of Light* and appears as a contributing theme in numerous short stories. Incest is the single most important motif in Oates' fiction, and the analytic model developed in this chapter allows its interpretation as the exploratory operation of the attempt to define and achieve power.

The slot at the top of the diagram refers to the broad project of Oates' fiction to recover or recreate an ideal balance of power and nurture. The last two chapters address this utopian objective. Chapter 7 summarizes Oates' overall project of the reformation of the family as it unfolds in *Bellefleur* and *Marya*. Jameson's object is to approach what, with reference to Freud's concept of the personal unconscious, he styles the "political unconscious" that motivates literary production. Similarly Chapter 7 defines the *feminist unconscious* implied through Oates' patterns of refusal and transgression as the motivation of resistance in all her work.

The final chapter moves beyond the dialectics of refusal and transgression *within* Oates' texts to consider Oates' dialectic *with* the text by analyzing the narrative figure of "The Transgressive Other." Noting that this character has been present throughout Oates' oeuvre, the discussion focuses on its predominance in Oates' most recent novels: *American Appetites*, *Soul/Mate*, and *Because It Is Bitter, and Because It Is My Heart*. Concluding that "The Transgressive Other" introduces the central tension between the investment in and the resistance to family ideology in Oates' fiction, the chapter ends by summarizing the specific components of Joyce Carol Oates' feminist accomplishment.

Family historian Rayna Rapp insists that we must "deconstruct the family as a natural unit, and reconstruct it as a social one." During the process, she predicts, "we'll find one very important aspect of the family is ideological. As such, its very meaning becomes a terrain of struggle" (239). For Oates, the relationships within the modern family provide the site of such ideological struggle; the Jamesonian overview of this study provides a map of its demanding terrain. To chart its features—the striking configuration of refusals and transgressions—and to trace the confusions and conflicts of its array of characters and plots as nodal points in a vast landscape reveals the larger pattern in Joyce Carol Oates' domestic fiction: the impetus toward reformation of the American family and the detrimental ideologies of gender and power it perpetuates.

Chapter One

Mothers and Fathers: The Demotion of the Ideal

The initial move in Joyce Carol Oates' domestic fiction is the demotion of the mythic Mother and Father to the ordinary mother and father, a demotion usually inscribed in contrast to the omnipotence of former deities. To understand this contrast it is helpful to distinguish the operation of three levels of experience. *Reality* may be said to include all of the determinant facts of the social and economic order in which the narrative occurs; inaccessible to the characters, it provides the background for Oates' family analysis. In the foreground of Oates' accounts the next two levels operate. *Ideality* serves the ideological aspirations of her characters; it provides the allusive pattern for what should, but cannot be. In Oates' works the ideal is often indicated through mythic references; mothers and fathers may bear traces of lost distinction: goddesses of the ancient earth and the Judeo-Christian God-the-Father combine as primal parents of a lost Eden. In conflict with this level of nostalgia, Oates presents the level of graphic *actuality*, which contains the characters' often extreme responses to problematic experience. The operation of all three levels is well represented in an early story, "The Census Taker," which pits the census taker, a city man who has faith in the rules and signs of a protective order, against a thoroughly existential little country girl.

Although the census is sanctioned as a means of documenting reality, both the unnamed census taker and Rose Ann Robins, the daughter of the household, admit the impossibility of approaching the real. In the absence of the father, the designated "head of the family" (*By the North Gate* 33), whom the census taker waits to interview, Rose Ann turns the tables by asking him loaded questions. When he agrees that the purpose of the census is to count the number of residents of the area, she argues that during the two years it takes to accomplish the count its information has become invalid: "Half of them people you got in that book are dead now or grown old or different." The census taker recognizes in her remark the expression of his own "secret fear, his secret horror." He had often been afraid "that each new entry in this official book negated an earlier entry, that the columns of names, dates, places were absurd" (34).

The census, stripped of its claims to reality, is evidently only a projection of ideality. The census taker comforts himself with the notion that when he returns to the city and delivers "the book to the proper authorities" it would "become real, would have a greater reality than any arbitrary juxtaposition of human lives out here in the country" (35). The census, then, is meant to secure a consoling illusion that will contradict frightening experience. Like the "signs" (36) that can warn of approaching storms, it is a part of an ideal and imposed order meant to secure the safety of the city man. The country girl, however, recognizing the restriction of con-forming to predetermined ideality, opposes it with an attentive report of felt experience on the level I am calling actuality. She refuses the circum-scribed and foreordained existence she suggests that the census perpetu-ates: "no numbers writ down in a book to stand for me."

I ain't goin' through the old ways—not comin' from a child to a woman, havin' children to keep on with the old ways, sufferin' them, sufferin' all agony to squeeze them out in no walled-in world. An' sick all your life, an' poor. (37–38)

As a stay against the ruthless experiential view of family presented by the girl, whom the census taker identifies as mad (39), he clutches an idealized image of "back home," a treasured snapshot of "the house and part of the beach" that was "taken long ago" (38), to which he wishes to retreat.

As "The Census Taker" reveals, the family in Oates' fiction cannot be absolutely known or located in terms of the real but must be inferred in the gap between the ideal and the actual as presented through the conflicts of her characters. The dual register of idealization and actuality apparent in this story is also a consistent feature of the presentation of women.

According to *The Larousse Encyclopedia of Mythology*, the composite figure of the Great Goddess combined the attributes of fertility and absolute power. Plants, animals, seasons, human beings, and the stars and planets—all were subject to the Goddess's control: "mistress of life, she was also sovereign of death" ("The Great Goddess" 87). The titles of two of Oates' works make it apparent that they are to be read against expectations evoked by this archetype. In *Cybele*, for example, the Asiatic goddess of love narrates the story of the decline of Edwin Locke, "a lover of mine who worshipped me, and became careless with his life, which was soon taken from him—more abruptly than I would have liked, and more cruelly; for I came to pity him in the end" (11). The novel demonstrates that the strength and purity of the goddess could not be safely admitted to the suburban actuality of the unfortunate Locke. *The Goddess and Other Women* also contains stories that evoke aspects of this archetype only to portray its destructive insertion into modern life.

In "Concerning the Case of Bobby T.," "Blindfold," and "Small Avalanches," young girls discover the power of their own developing sexuality, a power that has destructive consequences rather than positive effects in each story. At the level of ideality women possess passion and force, which, operating within the opportunities of expression their society provides, are experienced at the level of actuality as ambiguous or immoral.

Certainly this is the case in "Ruth," another story from *The Goddess and Other Women*. Ruth, a young woman whose mother is dying, is taken in for the summer by her aunt's family, the Wreszins. Quiet and passive, Ruth nonetheless has a powerful and uncanny effect on Mr. and Mrs. Wreszin, accountable only in terms of the ideality she represents to each of them. The Wreszins are very similar to the family presented in "Swamps." The father, whose family farm has gradually deteriorated, is discontent in his factory job, and the traditional mother is much occupied, like the mother in the earlier story, with preserving the fruit that their acreage still yields. Indeed, the Wreszins live beside "a great mile-long swamp" that had suddenly and unaccountably replaced the forest that had previously flourished there, but highway construction had

somehow blocked off its drainage—a process so utterly mysterious that it could not be explained to people in the area—and out of nowhere a rich, thick scum had risen, slowly, and for some inexplicable reason the trees had begun to die, dying from the inside, choked. (85)

At night the din of the insects and frogs that inhabit the decaying country lend it an aspect of vitality, but by day it "appeared sullen, ugly, dead, as if its secret life had retreated beneath the gray scum and could wait" (85–86).

In this metaphoric setting, Ruth becomes the symbolic repository for the lost secret life. When Mr. Wreszin first meets her, Ruth confides that she has had an illegitimate child. What he perceives in this confession of experience, however, is evidence of her extraordinary innocence that "made him innocent too" (92). Ruth, presented through an iconography of gardens, can impart an innocence, an appreciation of the flawed landscape akin to that of Eden before the Fall: "It's like a garden here," she tells him happily, noticing the "profusion" of trees and bushes in the area around the house, and through her eyes, Wreszin seems to see his world again in a new way. He hides "his face against Ruth overcome with gratitude" (104).

Both Mr. and Mrs. Wreszin attempt to use Ruth to gain access to a past, to a potential in themselves that they had never actually possessed: "Mrs. Wreszin tried to recall herself as a girl, before her marriage, but could not. . . . But she liked to imagine that she had been like Ruth" (96). Mr. Wreszin believes that Ruth allows him to recover a secret and essential self: "what was really him." Her presence relieves him of what is "accidental and ugly" in his own life—his social, geographic, historical, economic situation—and ushers him into a pastoral "world of birds and animals with pulsating throats that hid in the fields, and to the constant movement of the sun and the moon, belonging to everyone and no one" (104).

Mrs. Wreszin brushes Ruth's hair, dressing it in ribbons, as if she is adorning the lost goddess in herself. Mr. Wreszin makes love to Ruth in the open air, and when she announces her pregnancy, plans to run away with her. On the occasion of their escape, however, the daylight identity and the nighttime self of Mr. Wreszin grapple in deadly conflict. In the car, facing a future, "knowing no names for anything and ashamed of nothing," Wreszin suddenly feels as if "he had left something behind but could not remember it" (107). The result of this crisis of opposed sentiments, this conflict of ideality and actuality, is an automobile accident in which Wreszin dies instantly, leaving the terrified Ruth to babble defensively to the people who discover the wreck: "Why—why—it isn't my fault" (108).

At the level of ideality Ruth is definitively an earth goddess, which in Oates' fiction denies her a place in the actuality the Wreszins—he a taciturn middle-aged man "beginning to go to fat but careful to hide it" (86) and his wife a woman with a life "so empty that real news dazzled her and she didn't know how to talk about it" (88)—clearly represent. The level of reality of this account is inaccessible. Like the lost forest after the emergence of the mysterious swamp, the "farmers" have been "dispossessed by obscure economic changes—and their sons who joked and punched one another and didn't seem yet to be aware of their condition" (86).

"Ruth" outlines the failure of ideality as it is experienced in Oates' family fiction. The misunderstood pressures generated by real economic conditions are inadequately organized by ideal projections, and actuality registers the terrible crash of the conflict. The initiating gesture in Oates' oeuvre is a mythic reference to plenitude—for women, some hint of the Universal Goddess—that at the level of actuality the text invariably challenges. This tendency, evident in the stories of young women in *The Goddess and Other Women*, is even more conspicuous in Oates' portrayals of mothers.

THE GREAT MOTHER GONE TO SEED

In the title story "The Goddess," Claudia discovers among the discarded bric-a-brac of a rundown gallery "a curious Oriental statuette." As she stares, the little icon "pot-bellied, naked, her breasts long and pointed, her savage fat-cheeked face fixed in a grin, her many arms outspread" turns "slowly into the figure of a woman" (401). This transfiguration from goddess to woman is typical of the presentation of mothers in Oates' fiction.

Arlene Bartlett of *Childwold*, for example, epitomizes The Great Mother gone to seed. Resident of the same deteriorating rural environment as the Wreszins, Arlene, happy with her numerous illegitimate children, is a woman who dreams of pregnancy as a sensuous and blurred state of satisfaction, waking depressed to an empty womb. Although she is an occupant of the upstate area Oates has ironically dubbed Eden County, Arlene's dominant attributes—sexuality and maternity—are dishonored in the fallen world: "*Your mother is a...D'you know what your mother is?*" school children taunt (82). The contraction of the power of the former goddess of fertility is evident in a scaled-down description of her maternal domain. Arlene is described as fussing over a poinsettia plant, "a living thing" that "had to be tended" (139–40).

A much less sympathetic instance of this demotion is the presentation of Grandma Wendall in *them*. "So tall, she seemed to see farther than most people" (55); "very knowing . . . the old woman's eyes, fixed upon what was young and therefore helpless in Loretta, knowing how to seek it out" (56); with features reminiscent of a baleful icon, with "a head like a statue's head, a marvelous ugly brow, sharp green eyes" (57)—Grandma Wendall is more than a domineering mother-in-law. The diction initially confers on her the status of a malevolent goddess: she is all-seeing, all-knowing, and all-powerful, a status rescinded by a later scene. After the death of her son, an aging and dependent Grandma Wendall must make her home with her daughter-in-law's family. Sick of the elderly woman's dictatorial demands and disparagement, on one occasion when Grandma Wendall orders her granddaughters to help her to the bathroom, rebellious Betty shoves her roughly out the back door: "Let her go in her pants! She's all dirty anyway, the old bag, the old bitch!" (149). The helpless human weakness of the old woman at this moment illustrates the degradation of female potential in Oates' mothers.

The most extensive treatment of this pattern of degradation is presented in *A Garden of Earthly Delights*. In this work the only realization of mythic stature is the ironic reference of the title to Hieronymous Bosch's triptych that portrays the creation and subsequent loss of the earthly paradise. Like the family in "Swamps" and the Wreszins in "Ruth," the Walpoles of *A Garden of Earthly Delights* are victims of mysterious economic reversals. Unlike the other families, however, who still cling tenuously to hereditary gardens, the Walpoles have lost their farm. Cast forever from their personal Eden, they traverse the country as migratory fruit pickers, harvesting a bounty that does not sustain them. Carleton, the father, remembers a photograph of himself and his bride, Pearl, "standing by the side of the good barn" (20) as an image of ideal fulfillment, precious, and inaccessible:

he would be surrounded . . . the warm . . . familiar faces of his family and relatives, and his dream might open up suddenly . . . to show him the back garden, the side orchard, the barnyard with its rich-smelling hay stack, the barn itself—everything! (21)

In the novel, the "pretty but fragile" lost bride of the photograph (20) is replaced by an angry, sick woman who grows increasingly "sleepier, slower to recover" after the birth of each child (23). When Pearl Walpole finally dies, it is off-stage, as if it is an event so inevitable that it does not have to be noted in the text. This inevitability is further emphasized in the decline of Nancy, Carleton's next companion. In the beginning, young Nancy is carefree and enthusiastic. During her first pregnancy, however, she becomes petulant and unaccountably aged: "Clara saw that her face was creased with tiny wrinkles" (73). Mary Lou Parrott concludes that the examples of Pearl and Nancy teach Clara, the protagonist of the work, that the "physicality" of pregnancy is a "reminder of an inescapable predicament" of mental deterioration, denial of reality, aging, and death (51).

But to read Oates' mothers in terms of biological determinism is to miss the complex social insertion of her families. The way out of the maternal predicament is not the reformation of nature but the transgression of gender. Mrs. Mueller, "The Giant Woman" of the story of that title, exemplifies one form of this tactic. She is not a protagonist, but the focus of a legend: "Many years ago, in the foothills of the Chautauqa Mountains, where the north fork of the Eden River flows into the wide, flat Yew Creek, there lived a giant woman" (*Night-Side* 204).

Around this monumental figure local gossip weaves two strains of rumor. The first is of great concern to the little girl who is the protagonist of the story, a child who suffers being the younger and timid sister of the supercilious Donna. Mrs. Mueller, once "at least six feet five inches tall" and "nearly two hundred and fifty pounds at her heaviest" and still a figure of terror to the local children, is reputed to have hidden large sums of money in her house, which they dare one another to try and locate. As the children rummage through her musty junk and old linen, the younger sister does indeed discover a great cache of stiff, new bills of high denominations. But she keeps this knowledge from the others, letting the money remain hidden and leaving the old woman's house feeling inexplicably "happy" (220) and carefree.

As readers, we expect that the imputed wealth will turn out to be fantasy, that the children will certainly discover how weak is the basis for the old woman's awesome reputation. Instead, Oates repairs the little girl's sense of her own weakness through a tale that uncovers the legitimate basis of power: money. But such power has a price. Mrs. Mueller is explicitly masculine, and the second strain of local rumor recounts that she is the antithesis of a nurturing mother: "They said she was like a murderer. . . . Donna said it was her little boy, just my age; the old woman had let him die somehow and hadn't even told people about it" (206). In the strictly gendered world of Oates' family fiction, to acquire the male prerogative of power is to sacrifice feminine identity.

Oates confided in an interview with Linda Kuehl that she has "great admiration for those females who I know from my own life, my background, my family—very strong female figures who do not have much imagination in an intellectual sense" but who are "very capable of dealing with life" (308). This admiration of female strength, as in the story "The Giant Woman," is confined in her fiction to the context of legend, most often finding expression in Oates' treatment of mothers in terms of a nostalgia that is confounded by actuality. Her interest in this theme and situation may account for her enthusiasm for Harriette Arnow's *The Dollmaker*: "There are certainly greater novels . . . but I can think of none that have moved me more" (608). In her review Oates particularly praised the first scene of Arnow's novel:

The Dollmaker begins magnificently on a Kentucky road, with Gertie in her own world, knowing her strength, having faith in her audacity—a big, ungainly, ugly woman astride a mule, ready to force any car that comes along to stop for her. She is carrying her son Amos, who is dangerously ill, and she must get a ride to town in order to take him to a doctor. Her sheer animal will, her stubbornness, guarantee the survival of her son; she is not afraid to cut his flesh with a knife in order to release his pus. She succeeds in stopping a car with an army officer in it and she succeeds in overwhelming this man by the determination of her will. But it is her last success: after the novel's beginning, everything goes downhill for Gertie. ("Joyce Carol Oates on Harriette Arnow's *The Dollmaker*" 603)

The best way of approaching Oates' inaugural presentation of mothers is to understand that in her novels we never witness the narrative presentation of Gertie's first and last unqualified success. This moving moment when strength and nurturance are mutually compatible qualities of the archetypal mother is not merely passing but already past; it is confined to the peripheral references I have been defining as ideal. One of the most important accomplishments of her second novel, *A Garden of Earthly Delights*, is to establish as basic to Joyce Carol Oates' family fiction this fall from Mother to mother. *With Shuddering Fall*, Oates' first novel, is similarly concerned with the demotion of Father to father.

THE GENDER PACT

Both fathers and mothers are affected by the fall from mythic gardens to symbolic swamps. The special terror of the father is the subject of "Upon the Sweeping Flood," the title story appearing at the conclusion of Oates' second collection. In this story the overgrown Edenic gardens coexisting with the postlapsarian swamps of earlier stories are brutally superseded when thirty-nine-year-old Walter Stuart—steady and conservative in outlook, "district vice-president for one of the gypsum mills" (206)—gets caught in an Eden County hurricane.

On the way home from his own father's funeral, Stuart attempts to aid a boy and a girl who are also without a father. The eighteen-year-old girl is earthy, coarse, and transgressive, whereas the thirteen-year-old boy is terrified, puny, and given to intermittent fits of insanity. This trio is literally immersed in the existential onset of a swamp. Together the temporary family must take shelter during the night against the rising flood waters, first in the children's house, then clinging to the roof while the current washes over them, and in daylight on nearby high ground.

Traditionally, this plot would describe the little family protecting one another against the elements. "Upon the Sweeping Flood," however, evokes this expectation only to refute it. The apocalyptic immersion of the family is a baptism that transforms only Stuart. On the morning after the storm, something in the words and manner of the boy strangely disturbs him: "in that instant Stuart saw everything. He saw the conventional dawn that had mocked the night had mocked his desire to help people in trouble; he saw beyond that, his father's home emptied now even of ghosts" (223).

At this moment of epiphany, the boy, energetically brandishing a stick, chases one of the snakes that have also crawled onto the high ground, yelling, " 'I'll get you! I'll get you!' This must have been the sign Stuart was waiting for" (223). Using first a stick, then a stone, then his bare hands, Stuart strikes, then drowns the boy. As he lunges toward the girl, intending to rip off her clothes, a rescue boat arrives. "Save me!" Stuart cries (224).

This crisis occurring at the death of the Father and necessitating his replacement by a plainly deficient father contrasts two definitions of family: the ideal family of Stuart's lost life—"Stuart thought of his wife at home, walking through the rooms, waiting for him; he thought of his daughters in their twin beds, two glasses of water on their bureau....But these people knew nothing of him: in his experience now he did not belong to them" (217)—and the actual melange of the weak, puling boy, energized only by the prospect of violent aggression, who appears to strike Stuart as an aspect of himself that must be suppressed, and the girl, Stuart's strangely appealing though despicable Other, who must be raped and subdued.

Set in Oates' ironically titled "Eden County," the collection *Upon the Sweeping Flood*, which culminates in this story, presents the family after the collapse of primary Power, caught between two domestic orders—irrelevant ideality and chaotic actuality—neither of which is adequate. We witness the fall of the ideal Father and the predicament of the actual father facing the contingent and mutable nature of his own assertion of power. In fact, nine of the eleven stories in this volume portray fathers as absent or declining. The operation of the ideology of gender at this painful juncture is most fully expressed in Joyce Carol Oates' first novel *With Shuddering Fall*.

In a recent article Oates defined a favorite mode in her fiction as "realistic allegory" ("When Characters From the Page Are Made Flesh on the Screen" B1). Such allegory is evident in the opening chapter of the novel, in which Karen Herz is forced to accompany her father on a deathbed visit to "old Rule" (8). Like the Grandfather in "Swamps," Rule occupies a cabin on the periphery of a more modern world. Also, like the Grandfather's, his independence—his first words to his visitors are "Get out of here" (9)—is ineffectual and anachronistic, a fact symbolized by the decaying condition of his junk-strewn cabin:

Karen remembered a time years ago when Rule had tried to sort out his junk.
. . . But apparently he had given up and all piles . . . dissolved into one great,
insane pile of debris: to look at it was to invite a sensation of madness. (8)

It is the task of "Rule" to create order out of the bales of wire, piles of
cardboard, heaps of used lumber, and other accumulated trash, all the
encroaching effluvia of the industrial world. But he has apparently failed;
simple assertions of control have declined into "old Rule," and his death
will install mis-Rule in his place. For Karen to witness this dissolution of
power is to risk derangement, yet her father upbraids her for displaying
her confused emotions. There is nothing to be upset about, he explains:
"It will be Rule first, then me second in a few years, and then you too—one
thing you can be damn sure of" (13).

The theme of the book articulated by Karen's father—the destructive
inevitability of time—is conventional. What is interesting and unconven-
tional in Oates' first novel is her focus on Karen's crisis reaction to this
commonplace. Karen is so shaken by the visit that she sinks into a kind of
delirium—"Everything seemed to have happened in a dream" (13).

This first chapter emphasizes gender assignment. Karen is in the
cabin, the first paragraph declares, only because "her father would not
go alone carrying food; that was woman's work" (7). Man orders, woman
nourishes. But the soup Karen carries is kicked over to form a dark and
useless wet patch on the rough floor. If nurturance is not the issue in this
work, power is. As in the case of the two grandfathers and two father
figures of "Swamps," the complex articulation of power is divided
among the male characters. Old Rule represents inadequate force; mis-
Rule, Rule's son Shar, stands for anarchic force. He is a competitive
driver who has sped out of Karen's static and pastoral world to the
turbulent universe of race tracks and race riots. Karen's father, Mr. Herz,
an influential landowner, the most powerful man in the book because of
his connection with the economic sources of authority, attempts to
dominate both old Rule and the destructive upstart mis-Rule. But despite
Herz' position of apparent strength, old Rule's condition makes Karen
aware of her own father's weakness: old Rule's hair is black despite his
age, but Herz' is already flecked with gray. Karen's panic at her father's
threatened vulnerability is the key to the novel, and her subsequent
actions are all attempts to re-establish the certainty of his protection. All
the murky action of the narrative must be understood with regard to this
symbolic objective.

According to Elizabeth Dalton's dismissive summary of that action:

Karen, a beautiful seventeen-year-old girl, runs away from her respectable Catholic family with a racing driver, a brutal demon lover type who hits her father on the head with a rifle butt, takes Karen's virginity in some unspecified but degrading way, later has intercourse with her so violently that she has a miscarriage, and finally, driven wild by their helpless passion, smashes his car into a wall. Karen runs bleeding into the street where a race riot touched off by her lover's death is in progress. After a few months in a mental hospital, Karen is received back into her family; the book ends with Karen at Mass praying for forgiveness. (75)

That the issue of the father's power is at the core of Karen's frenetic history is laid bare by Oates' association of Mr. Herz with God's injunction to Abraham to sacrifice Isaac. After the brutal confrontation between Shar and Karen's father, Herz charges Karen: "Don't come to me until you get him. Kill him. Kill him" (50). Karen had been very moved when her father had read the parable from Genesis the Sunday before his encounter with Shar, a scene Oates refers to in an interview with Linda Kuehl four years after the publication of *With Shuddering Fall*, which she considers a "religious work" that is strictly parallel to the Old Testament account (309).

Like the Old Testament story, this work does concern a test of faith, but there the strict parallelism ends. God's authority is absolute, Abraham's faith is genuine, so Isaac is spared. In Oates' homily, however, we have already observed that Herz' patriarchal power is human and contingent. The shock of Rule's impending death initiates a conflict in Karen. One moment she is confiding to a would-be lover: "I want to love—to love—I want to live." But at the next moment she withdraws, exclaiming, "I've got to get home . . . My Father—I have to do something with my father" (22). Karen is both drawn to Shar and dependent on her father. Her faith is at best ambivalent.

Precisely because the authority in question is limited and the faith uncertain, the Isaac figure must be sacrificed. Karen's unwillingness to fully love Shar impels his destruction. The realization that he "had not yet violated Karen's secrecy" (174), as evidenced by her silence about her pregnancy, causes Shar to smash his car into a retaining wall. His death fulfills Herz' commandment, as commentator Ellen Friedman has observed,[1] but if Oates' story is parallel to the biblical account, the mysterious death of another Isaac figure, Karen's unborn child, must also signify. In "The Hostile Sun," a study of the poetry of D. H. Lawrence, the writer to whom *With Shuddering Fall* is most indebted, Oates analyzes Ursula's miscarriage at the end of *The Rainbow* as absolution from Skrebensky's child, "which is to her and to Lawrence hardly more than a symbol of the finite, the deathly personal and limited" (59).[2] The death of Karen's child, then, may signal her abandonment of her own potential—personal, finite (and inevitably deathly)—the apparently terrifying sexual impulse to leave home, mate, and create her own family.

Such a move would require courage, independence, a belief in the possibility of her own autonomy, qualities reserved for sons in the gender system of Oates' fiction. Karen, however, well trained as a daughter, realizes she has "no existence without the greater presence of someone to acknowledge her (her father; God)" (111). With absolutely no belief in her own strength and terrified at the adult realization that her protective father's might is human rather than ideal, Karen substitutes magic for growth in an attempt to repair the absolute power of Herz. She may be "insane" as Max accuses (192–193) and as her breakdown attests, but Karen's story represents an extreme example of the cultural insanity evident in all Oates' families.

In the initial scene an allegorical item is just visible under old Rule's deathbed: a rusty trap. The image recurs in Max's outraged accusations: "an insane trap. . . . And . . . look what it's done to you! Your insides drained out on a dirty bed, a mattress soaked with blood!" (192). The trap in Oates' fallen families must be understood as more than the twin traps of time and biology: it is the social trap of gender. The content of the gender pact is the agreement that if the female will always be weak, the male will always be strong, and that together they will collude to eliminate any force, experience, or development that would overturn this static assertion.

Oates remarked to Linda Kuehl that she finds thinking of this under-graduate novel "disturbing" ("An Interview with Joyce Carol Oates" 309). What bothers her may be Karen's cooperative capitulation to the self-de-structive demands of the gender pact. At the end of the book, having executed her terms of the bad bargain, Karen returns to the Herz household. Her lover dead, her child wilfully miscarried, Karen has recovered from her nervous breakdown, but Mr. Herz, who has recently had a stroke, has begun the inevitable slide into weakness and failure that no magic cove-nant can prevent.

Gayle Rubin distinguishes between biological fathers and societal patriarchs on the basis of power: "Abraham was a Patriarch—one old man whose absolute power over wives, children, herds and dependents was an aspect of the institution of fatherhood as defined in the social group in which he lived" (168). Oates casts Herz as a latter-day patriarch: he has dominion over land and numerous hired men and especially over children and women. "A passel of kids your father got over there," Shar comments.

"He wore out three women with it. Or was it four?" (39). But even Herz' power is limited by his mortality.

The most striking "shuddering fall" of the novel may be Mr. Herz' demotion from biblical Patriarch to flesh-and-blood daddy, but the problems presented by that fall are, in the focus of the work, Karen's. They are Herz (hers) in the rather broad name puns of the novel.

The problem with the gender pact is that it doesn't work. As ideology it can alter only perception, not actuality. Karen's father, she understands in the last pages of the work, is not an invincible patriarch, but "a cruel, ignorant old man who has always disguised himself with strength . . . like a shell you find by a swamp, turned over on its back and wriggling in the mud, trying by the ferocious charm of its eyes to avoid the stroke of death" (222). By withholding herself emotionally from Shar to support her father's disguise of strength, Karen has not only murdered Shar in the symbolic structure of the story, she has cooperated in the destruction of her own potential. As Oates explained to Kuehl,

With Shuddering Fall was conceived as a religious work where the father was the father of the Old Testament who gives a command as God gave to Abraham . . . and how we can obey it, and if we do obey it, we're not going to get rewarded for it anyway. . . . One has defeated the world and defeated one's own impulses and passions and is left with nothing—sort of like a nun. (309)

"I think there is probably a great deal that I am not owning up to" was Oates' preface to the above remarks. What Oates has not owned up to is the explicit theme of the social regulation of female sexuality that, more than religion, seems to be the concern of the book.

The problem of religion as Karen experiences it, as well as the problem of gender, is that it is practiced within the family—a family dependent Karen needs to be a part of. On the one hand, although Karen can recognize Mr. Herz in the last scene as "a killer" who "has no right to my life," on the other, she acknowledges, "But he is my father . . . and I love him." Karen's resignation to the ideological pact of the novel is clarified by her intention in the church service at the close of the novel to participate in the "communion" of others—"whatever experience they shared—whatever mystery it was. She recognized her home, her place. . . . It is insane to look for the meaning in life, and it is insane not to; what am I to do?" (223).

What Oates' first novel presents through Karen's story is what Terry Eagleton describes as the unexamined "complex structure of fear, desire, aggression, masochism and anxiety" (149–150) that keeps the gender system in place. The patterns of refusal and transgression in Oates' subsequent fiction are an attempt to answer Karen's disturbing initiating question.

THE BROKEN BOND

Oates' earliest works mark the passing of an old order: pagan goddesses and Old Testament patriarchs fall—turn into flawed mothers and fathers. By the second novel, *A Garden of Earthly Delights*, Eden is truly lost; the ideality Karen bargained to preserve in the first has truly vanished. Where Karen only visited the debased city of Synerdale, the migrant Walpoles must traverse a "Sin"-erdale that encompasses the whole United States, a demoted present that they are always visiting from an idealized past to which they can never return: "They talked for a while about 'going back,' " but they had lost all sense of what and where their lost "Kentucky" may have been (14).

But what may be even more important than the motif of expulsion from the pioneer garden into the sordid economy of the twentieth century is the terrifying deterioration of the archetypal parents and the resultant failure of their relationship.

As in "Swamps," Oates uses the occasion of birth—the quintessential instance of family continuity—to indicate that something is wrong. A traffic accident, rather than natural process, induces Pearl Walpole's labor, and on this occasion Carleton observes the dissolution of the bond between the couple: "There was this strange tie between them: they lived together, they slept together. They had lived together back home but that was a long time ago, did it have anything to do with now?" (17). At the moment of birth, Carleton longed for Pearl's death: "He had already killed Pearl, she had died somewhere on one of these highways or in some heat-drenched field" (19–20).

This sense of separation, the failure of cooperation, is the condition of parents in Oates' fallen world. Disjunction is the gender-defined relation of nurturance to power. Individual mothers and fathers are experienced by their families as flawed as a result of the suppression of gender qualities assigned to the other parent. Karen's understanding of her father purely in terms of his power is one such instance. And in *A Garden of Earthly Delights*, Clara is so aware of the life-destroying powerlessness of the maternal figures in her family that she chooses to attempt to secure power at the expense of nurturance.

"One always thinks of a few other people, day after day; there's no escape," Oates explained in an interview with Joe David Bellamy: "A father, a mother, a few beloved people—that is the extent of the universe emotionally. And if something goes wrong inside this small universe then nothing can ever be made right" (29). What has gone wrong in the small universe of the family Oates describes is the gender restriction of essential human qualities.

In an article on the source of fiction, Oates mentions "primitive force fields that generate 'theme' (or obsession!)" ("A Terrible Beauty Is Born. How?" 1). In the primitive force field of Oates' families the division of power and nurturance institutes gender-separate spheres of influence for mothers and fathers and sons and daughters, an arrangement experienced in contemporary society as dysfunctional. Joyce Carol Oates' earliest works register both nostalgia for the lost functional ideal and the recognition that the ideological gender pact that shapes the family system is corrupt and should be broken.

Chapter Two

Mothers and Daughters: The Refusal of Innocence

This chapter disputes denigrating critical assessments of the bad mothers and mad daughters of Oates' fiction by tracing the gradual development of the daughter from her earliest endeavor to distinguish herself as separate from her mother through the stages leading to her refusal of her mother's characteristic unexamined complicity in the social arrangement of female restriction. Our strategy will be to confront the assumptions that underlie such critical stereotypes by exploring Oates' complex articulations of mother and daughter roles and relationships.

Both Joanne Creighton and Mary Lou Parrott unequivocally conclude that Oates' mothers are bad mothers. In an influential article Creighton observes:

The Mothers—Clara of *A Garden of Earthly Delights*, Nada of *Expensive People*, Loretta of *them*, and Ardis of *Do with Me What You Will*—have all perfected the art of survival but at a cost to the people around them, their lovers and husbands and maladjusted children. They are cheerful and adjustable, egotistical and self-sufficient, feline and attractive, opportunistic and pragmatic, manipulative and amoral. ("Unliberated Women" 148).

Parrott's analysis adds *Childwold* to the works Creighton considers to conclude that in Oates' fiction "motherhood is perverted into a vehicle of feminine self-assertion utterly antagonistic to the needs of the child." Since "maternal authority is all the Oates mother can posit against social impotence and personal inadequacy," she "exploits love, she imposes guilt, she practices intimidation, she inflicts corporeal punishment, she uses psychological coercion, and she even poses as omniscient and omnipotent in order to control her child's thoughts and actions." Thus, "the quality of mothering that takes place in Oates' world is, at best, immature and, at worst, monstrously sadistic" (329).

The first problem with this commentary is that these generalized composite portraits obscure important differences among Oates' mother-and-daughter relationships. The second is that to read Oates' family fiction as a condemnation of mothers (or a vilification of daughters) is to miss the broader concern: the problematic insertion of women, both mothers and daughters, into a gender-restrictive culture.[1] Oates' mothers may attempt to deal with inadequate paternal power by the exploitative behavior Parrott describes, or they may accept their limitations with the plucky resiliency Creighton observes. The problem Oates' work addresses is, however, not motherhood, but power. And in her fiction it is the task of the daughters to develop consciousness of this problem.

This chapter defines domestic relation in Oates' works not with the static ideological labels of good and bad but with regard to dynamic descriptions of family psychology. D. W. Winnicott proposes the interactive concept of the "good-enough" mother, whose success may be measured through her child's progress toward autonomy. According to Winnicott, a good-enough mother is able to help her infant experience the capacity to manipulate people and objects. She is also able to support the infant's attendant need to experience separation from the mother without the anxiety that genuine separation would create (70–71).

Not an absolute standard, good-enough mothering is a general description of interaction that promotes the self-sufficiency of the child. Winnicott stresses that although the initial conditions of this relationship occur in infancy, they recur in later family situations, especially adolescence, the focus of Oates' mother-daughter narratives. Winnicott's model is particularly useful in the study of Oates' narratives because of the shared emphasis in his theory and her fiction on the issue of autonomy. But whereas Winnicott describes the conditions necessary for autonomy, Oates raises doubts about its possibility. For if the gender system of Oates' fiction precludes power as an attribute of mothers and daughters, to what extent can the mother-daughter relation foster the development of autonomy? Can Oates' mothers ever be good enough?

Instead of a simple negative answer, Oates' fiction demonstrates the gradual development of the consciousness of the daughters in relationships that extend from those Winnicott would describe as not good enough (145) to good enough. At one extreme, mothers suppress nurturance in the effort to achieve the self-sufficiency gender restriction denies them; at the other, they may struggle to nurture adequately despite financial, educational, and social limitations. The daughters' difficult approaches to autonomy in these different situations contain a common element: the evolution of the refusal of their mothers' uncontemplated innocence of the conditions that restrict them.

In the child's gradual development toward autonomy, Winnicott notes ascending levels from absolute dependence to total independence: extreme dependence, dependence, dependence-independence, independence-dependence, independence, and the capacity to adapt to the needs of others without sacrificing personal identity. The highest level is marked by the achievement of autonomy, whereas the lowest is defined by total physical neglect resulting in the death of the child. The inadequacies and talents of Oates' mothers tend to cluster at the middle levels of this continuum. For example, at the level designated as "independence," there is "an internalized environment: an ability on the part of the child to look after . . . herself." Any defect in the mother's care at this point is "not necessarily harmful." This is the situation in *Childwold*. Arlene Bartlett may be regarded as a good-enough mother; Laney's failures and successes supersede her mother's capacity for intervention.

The level "independence-dependence" is characterized by the child's experiments toward independence with an accompanying need to experience the security of dependence. The relationship between Loretta and Maureen Wendall, the mother and daughter in *them*, exemplifies this intermediate level. Maureen's attempts at independence are half-hearted and wrong-headed, whereas Loretta's protection is inadequate; her maternal skill lies between not good enough and good enough.

The mother and daughter of *Do with Me What You Will*, however, are a definitive example of a not-good-enough relationship. At the stage of a "dependence" Winnicott claims, "conditions that fail do in fact traumatize, but there is already a person there to be traumatized." At the next level, as well, the child's tentative gestures of independence need much protection. The novel demonstrates failures at both these levels, which may, according to Winnicott, result in serious problems: affective disorders, antisocial tendencies, or pathological dependence (66–67). Daughter Elena's condition in the early chapters of *Do with Me What You Will*, which heralds severe mental disturbance marked by deep dependency, makes her subsequent healthy development remarkable and marks the first tentative step in the Oates daughter's advancement toward autonomy.

THE DAUGHTER'S SEPARATION

In order to analyze the pathological mother-daughter relation in *Do with Me What You Will* we turn to Gregory Bateson's concept of the "double-bind." This structure of severely inadequate parent-child connection requires several conditions: First, there must be a perpetrator, who is usually a mother, and there must be a victim, who is usually a child. Second, the situation must be frequently repeated, and, finally three characteristic negative injunctions are necessary:

1. The issuance of a primary injunction ("Don't criticize father, as he's the head of the household")
2. The issuance of a secondary and contradictory injunction ("We allow the children to speak their minds about us")
3. The issuance of a tertiary injunction requiring comment or participation ("What do you think about Dad?")

These injunctions may be articulated or implied, but the second injunction usually conflicts with the first in a differnt mode of communication, and the third injunction excludes the possibility of escape. All three of the injunctions are understood by the victim to be enforced by punishment or threats to survival.[2]

With this structure in mind let us examine a particularly telling passage in *Do with Me What You Will*. When Elena is nine years old, she works with her mother Ardis long hours under very bright lights as part of a mother-and-daughter modeling team. She is posed in stationary attitudes and ordered not to move and not to blink. Professionally trained never to respond in a natural manner, Elena is consistently rewarded for her compliance; she is complimented for being a good girl. Nevertheless, on one occasion when a new admirer has taken Ardis and Elena to a dimly-lit restaurant after a modeling session, Elena makes what seems to her a dangerous blunder: she stumbles against something in the semi-darkness, and her eyes begin to water. The man's notice of her condition prompts the following exchange between mother and daughter:

> "Why are you blinking like that?" Ardis asked
> "Her eyes must be sore," said the man.
> Elena did not answer. She waited. In a few minutes her mother would forget, would turn away; she could rely on that. But for some reason Ardis slid her arm around Elena's shoulders, gently, and examined her eyes. It was very embarrassing because the man, a stranger, was watching. "Now tell the truth, honey. Can you see all right?"

"I don't know."

"Do your eyes burn?"

"A little." She did not try to squirm away from her mother, though she wanted to. She wanted to tell both her mother and this man that she was all right, it didn't matter. She hated them to look at her so directly.

"Elena, you should have said something up in the studio, if the lights were shining in your eyes," Ardis said. Elena did not know how to reply. She sensed something unusual in her mother's voice, a tone Ardis wouldn't use if they were alone. . . . So Elena didn't know what her mother wanted her to say. . . .

"I'm sorry," Elena said.

"You're a good little girl to sit so still," Ardis said, "but if this happens again you should tell me....Unless...unless you did it to be bad, to get out of work tomorrow....Was that the reason, Elena?"

"No."

"To make your eyes water and get red and ugly, so you wouldn't have to work tomorrow...? Elena, tell the truth. Was that it?"

"No," Elena said miserably." (62–63)

The injunctions of the double-bind imposed on Elena by Ardis in this scene are (1) the unspoken rule, "Never betray your natural responses, particularly if they will jeopardize my livelihood." In order to impress a new man with her maternal concern, however, Ardis issues a second injunction through her posturing solicitude: (2) "My child and I communicate openly and honestly." That this is not the case is evident in Elena's extraordinary wariness. Ardis' accusations, which break through her pose of concern at the end of the exchange, indicate that Elena is accurate in her perception of threat and punishment in the directly stated third injunction: (3) "Tell me the truth."

In *Inventing Motherhood* Ann Dally observes that the "normal child" manages to thwart or reject double-bind situations unless previous emotional experience makes the recurrence of any part of the double-bind ordeal unendurable (231–232). Elena's induction into this disturbed sequence was her abduction from her school playground by her estranged and mentally deranged father when she was seven years old. At his insistence Elena crawled under the fence into his erratic and abusive care, because, he explained, her mother was dead. After his suicide Elena is discovered evidently disoriented, half-starved, filthy, and covered with insect bites in a San Francisco rooming house. In addition to the fundamental unpredictability of an unreliable parent that unsettles Elena in the quoted example, the abduction introduces the symbolic register of Elena's confusion: a pattern of disguise and failure of recognition that is also characteristic of the relationship of Elena and her mother throughout the novel. Removing a wig and glasses a few blocks from the school, her father, Leo Carter, demanded, "Now you recognize me, don't you?" (22). But caught in the confusion of cross-purpose, it is a long time before Elena is able to recognize either parent.

In a California barroom Leo regaled the patrons with an account of Elena's mother's protean transformations. He could go to bed with a blonde and wake up next to a redhead; she could even rearrange her face. Model, adventuress, cocktail waitress, television personality, Ardis constantly changes her hair color, her make-up, even her name to complement her shifting roles. After the rescue, Elena awakens in a hospital room to a red-haired stranger, a mother whose identity eludes her throughout the novel.

On another occasion, Ardis, worried about money, goes out for the evening to return with a new hairdo, a new style of dress, a new man, and a new career. Elena is uncertain for a moment about whether the renovated woman who returns is really her mother. In a later instance, after Elena's marriage, she is introduced to a stranger at a cocktail party. After several moments of impersonal conversation, Elena is amazed to observe Marya Sharp's face turn into that of Ardis, her mother.

As in the episode in the twilit restaurant, Elena's eyes rather than Ardis' character appear to be at fault. Narcissistic, malevolently manipulative, even when her character seems most clearly revealed, Ardis manages to make Elena doubt her own ability to discern. Elena, for example, recalls Ardis' machinations before her daughter's marriage: "something about sleeping pills, you'd brought them home for me," so that Elena could "take an overdose if he didn't agree to our terms" (428). Yet when her mother disputes the veracity of this recollection, Elena immediately doubts her own perception. But more important than Elena's failure to recognize her mother is her consequent failure to perceive an identity of her own, a condition witnessed by her extreme passivity and evidenced by her inability to differentiate herself from Ardis when she contemplates an advertisement featuring the two of them:

Elena sat and gazed at the advertisement, first gazed at herself on the left—the sixteen-year-old who looked eighteen but who was really only fourteen—that is, Elena herself was fourteen—and then on the right, the thirty-nine-year-old woman who looked eighteen but who was really thirty-six, Ardis's true age. Sometimes she believed she was on the left, sometimes on the right. (76)

This failure has also been conditioned by Elena's initial trauma through Leo's drastic alteration of her own appearance. The black dye he used on

Elena's hair stained her neck and formed dark runnels at the sides of her face. The mistreated little girl the police discovered huddled fearfully under the covers of a dirty cot was no longer the beautiful child Leo had believed he would be willing to die for. In fact, he imagined that only death could repair her. If she died, he reasoned, her insect bites would vanish, and she would turn into "a perfect child again, her hair light-blond again, almost white, the color of angel's hair" (48).

According to Winnicott, adequate parenting encourages the development in the child of a spontaneous and individualized "True Self." When there is parental failure to provide "continuity," "reliability," and "graduated adaptation" (70–71) to the child's increasing independence, she develops, instead, a compliant "False Self" through which she "builds up a false set of relations" as a means of self-protection (146–147). What Leo's insanity originated—the destruction of the true self of Elena—Ardis' self-serving double-binds reinforce. Cleaning Ardis' apartment, cooking her food, or posing as her doll-size replica, Elena is an extreme example of the false self, a condition that, according to Harry Guntrip, results in "either tame goodness or criminality" (104).

"You," a story in which the outcome contrasts with *Do with Me What You Will*, divides the strategies of the false self—extreme rebellion or acquiescence—between the twin daughters of another narcissistic mother, movie star Madeline Randall. Crucial to this story as well is the project of the recognition of the mother, the importance of which is registered in the form, a dramatic monologue by acquiescent Marion. She traces events of a family crisis at home as simultaneous with her mother's activities in another city, a narrative strategy that, like the emphatically single voice of the monologue, serves to underscore the separation of mother and daughters. This separation is further accentuated by Marion's employment of second-person address. This form effects a linguistic distinction between the "you" of the mother and the "I" of the daughter. But at the climax of the story the assertion of separation, Marion's attempt to reclaim a "true self," is discounted in a scene of blurred recognition. A disheveled middle-aged woman disembarks from Madeline's returning flight, an ordinary woman Marion is eager to claim as mother. In the next instant, however, Madeline herself emerges, beautiful, imperious, still the magical figure of control Marion is unable to elude or resist. The movie-star mother seizes her daughter's wrist in a gesture of "absolute claim" to conclude the story by negating the insistent avowal of individuation in Marion's narrative style (*The Wheel of Love* 336).

"You" is instructive because it connects the act of accurate recognition of the mother with the daughter's attempt to actualize her true self. The story also points up the great difficulty of the project. We have every reason to expect that any similar project on Elena's part is also doomed to failure. The double-bind mother raises her children through an "infinite series of impossible dilemmas" in which they "can only avoid guilt or loss of love or support from the mother, or a direct confrontation with her hostility, by denying the evidence of their senses," (Dally 227). These children often exhibit symptoms of schizophrenia,[3] and indeed Elena shows evidence of disturbance that culminates in mental breakdown. It is all the more surprising, therefore, when, like the other troubled daughters who precede her, Karen Herz and Maureen Wendall, Elena manages a "self-cure."[4]

Disappointed in Oates' previous portrayals of passive women, Joanne Creighton discovered in Elena's story a message of female liberation to contrast with her portrait of the typical Oates Daughter:

All are fragile, quiet, insecure, introspective, and above all, vacuous. Opposed to the catlike agility of the Mothers, the daughters have little resilience and are incapable of dealing with the unexpected. All are skirting the edge of severe psychological disorder. ("Unliberated Women" 148–149)

I contend, however, that Elena's self-assertion is consistent with the attitudes of all of Oates' daughters. They do not merely skirt around madness; unlike their mothers, they must reluctantly confront and try to come to terms with the cultural situation that creates it. Creighton ascribes Elena's "successful liberation" to the intensity of a love affair, but although Elena's sexual awakening is undoubtedly an important factor in her growth, Oates' fiction customarily avoids the formula of a love-story resolution.

Instead, the best index of Elena's progress is the clear recognition of her mother in a two-page chapter at the end of the novel. Ardis-Marya has posted to Elena a plastic record with a message to "all my friends in Detroit and Michigan" to announce her latest marriage. Recognizing her mother's familiar voice, Elena played the message again and again, allowing herself to experience her pain: "she felt her eyes sting with a mysterious acrid throbbing; not exactly tears" until she no longer needed to hear it, "so she dusted it carefully with a soft chamois cloth and slid it back into its plain wrapper and filed it with Marvin's records" (459). Kathy Wexler comments that the way to break a double-bind involves giving yourself permission to recognize its contradiction and articulate its operation: "if the receiver of contradictory messages can acknowledge his confusion (a dangerous act in most families), the mystification disappears and so does the double-bind" (7). This chapter recounts such an act of demystification and consequent dismissal.

Females typically experience problems of self-definition, individuation, and separation, Nancy Chodorow argues in *The Reproduction of Mothering*, because of the predominance in our society of exclusive care by the mother in early childhood. Whereas boys differentiate themselves from domestic experience, seeking role definition through cultural models, "girls' identification processes are continuously embedded in and mediated by their ongoing relationship with their mothers" (176). Although family ideology sentimentalizes the closeness of the resulting bond, two centuries of popular women's fiction lead Sally McNall to an opposing opinion: "On the evidence of our American fiction, the problem has been . . . that growing up to be a mother has been each heroine's only alternative, and yet a dangerous, frightening, and difficult task." Gothic and sentimental fictions expose the "terror and rage" of

the girl child's inability to fully relinquish unintegrated fantasy images of her earliest love, her mother. Unable to accept the loss of the "good" mother, she searches endlessly to project her image onto another and recreate it in herself. Unable to believe that she can separate from the "bad" mother, she tries endlessly to propitiate or make reparation to projections of this image. Heroine after heroine, first seduced then abandoned, finally believing in romantic love, has avoided growing up by a retreat into madness or self-abnegation or trivia or flirtation with death. (121–122)

McNall defines the type of fiction that produces this immature heroine—gothic tales and love stories—as *romance*, a term that in her use indicates themes of emotional regression. In her typology, the novel is the form that resists such regression. Our consideration of Elena's achievement of individuation in *Do with Me What You Will* demonstrates that Oates is writing novels in this sense of the word. The Elena of the early part of the novel, pathologically dependent, locked by the double-bind into ceaseless propitiation of an inadequately understood projection of the "bad" mother, is a virtual parody of the heroine McNall describes. Essential to the separation and integration necessary for maturity is, according to McNall, "the completed process of mourning for . . . the mother of our child-minds and emotions, whom we must relinquish as we attempt to acquire adult minds and emotions" (9).[5] In the scene when Elena fully recognizes her mother as the artificial and distant voice of an impersonal greeting, she mourns Ardis and is able to literally put her away. In this act Elena refuses her previous self-abnegation and asserts her capacity for an adult mind and emotions, or, in Winnicott's phrase, a true self.

In her presentation of daughters, Oates frequently makes use of the stereotypical "romantic" heroine: she explicitly depicts justifiable passivity as an attribute psychologically appropriate to the actual treatment of the protagonist only in order to reject it. This rejection is accomplished in Oates' fiction through the daughters' resistance of propitiation of pathological mothers (or mother images), like Ardis of *Do with Me What You Will,* and their refusal of the unexamined, or innocent, internalizations of better mothers, like those in *them* or *Childwold.*

THE RAPE OF CONSCIOUSNESS

Unlike Elena, stalled for years at the first steps toward autonomy, most of Oates' adolescent daughters can differentiate themselves from mothers whom they clearly recognize. "Where Are You Going, Where Have You Been?" begins with this observation about the difference in appearance between a mother and a daughter that contrasts with the confusingly similar portraits[6] in *Do with Me What You Will*: "she knew she was pretty and that was everything. Her mother had been pretty once too, if you could believe those old snapshots in the album, but now her looks were gone and that was why she was always after Connie" (*The Wheel of Love* 29).

Oates' daughters at this stage of development share a fascination with their own faces evident in a tendency to study their reflections. Scenes of mirror gazing by Grace in "Pastoral Blood," the teenage Loretta in *them,* and Connie in "Where Are You Going, Where Have You Been?" precede the girls' initiation into a brutal male world. In his developmental model of the human subject, Jacques Lacan designates the "mirror-phase," which occurs before the child's insertion into the masculine symbolic order, as a key event. Somewhere between the ages of six and eighteen months the infant will spot its reflection in the mirror and identify a "self." Lacan emphasizes that this integrated image far exceeds the infant's genuine capacities and represents a projected image, an imaginary ideal. Kaja Silverman argues that, although Lacan would like to insist that the content of the reflection is "ideologically neutral," we "cannot interpret the reflection within which the child finds its identity too literally; it must be understood at least to some degree as a cultural construct" influenced by the mother's interpretation or mediated through the intervention of stories, games, and toys that "determine the way it will eventually regard itself" (160).

If this cultural contamination influences Lacan's child, it is a determinant factor for Oates' young women. Loretta, for example, combing her filmstar hairdo one evening realizes that peering into the mirror was like "looking into the future" (*them* 9). In the mirror-gaze of Oates' work, the psychological growth toward autonomous individuation is corrupted by an interposed image created by culture. Oates' heroines do not see themselves in the glass but discover faces of promise and crude perfection sketched by movies, advertising, and popular songs they risk safety to realize.

It is this culturally fashioned face, which fifteen-year-old Connie is constantly alert for, that forms the basis for her most salient mannerism, the "quick, nervous giggling habit of craning her neck to glance into mirrors or checking other people's faces to make sure her own was all right" (29). Commenting on the film version of "Where Are You Going, Where Have You Been?" Oates describes Connie as "an innocent young girl seduced by vanity; she mistakes death for erotic romance of a particularly American/trashy sort" ("When Characters from the Page" B1). The mirror of twenty-year-old Grace also returns a culturally defined image. Insisting that her very image is an artifact replicated and purveyed by mass media, she insists we recognize her as "a cheerleader" from the comics or the movies with the kind of hair that is used to sell shampoo in television commercials.

In "The Voyage to Rosewood," sixteen-year-old Marsha also comes to understand that the image in the glass exceeds her own identity. The threatening presence of a violent young man causes her to "dreamily" acknowledge "that what I have worked at sloppily and sluttishly before my bedroom mirror has been loosed into this strange winter day and the raw ovals of Ike's eyes" (*The Goddess and Other Women* 255).

The terrible irony of development as Oates stages it is that just at the point the adolescent girl moves toward a confident assessment of what she earnestly believes is her own individuality, events shatter this false image in the glass. The morning after Loretta descries her future in her face, her first lover lies dead, bleeding by her side, for no other reason than that her brother has acquired a gun and decided, "I'm going to kill somebody with it" (*them* 13). This violent event, not her own rosy reflection, determines her future.

The most direct influence on Oates' mirror symbolism is her fascination with the works of Lewis Caroll, which has carried over from her childhood into her teaching, her novels, and her critical work.[7] The looking glass of Oates' heroines, like that of Alice, defines a border between apparently safe and ordinary existence and a distorted and frightening world, as the adolescent girl moves from the stifling security of her mother's home to the elementary violence of the male sphere in Oates' fiction. The danger of this transition is often expressed in stories of imminent rape.

Marsha, for instance, of "The Voyage to Rosewood" feels "a sense of indefinable entrapment, imprisonment in a fluid and sweet and fragrant element" (244) in the love of her mother and two grandmothers. One morning while she is waiting for the school bus, the impression "of being here, safe, with everyone ordinary and predictable" is suddenly repugnant. Impulsively, she catches, instead, a commercial bus and heads for a small town she has never seen. "I am waking up without mercy or kindness," she realizes, "and leaving them all behind" (241). She is picked up in a country tavern by Ike, a commonplace version of the diabolical rapist Arnold Friend of "Where Are You Going, Where Have You Been?"

In "Pastoral Blood," Grace is motivated by the reified apathy of her mother's middle-class world. On the anniversary of her father's death, she withdraws 1,000 dollars from the bank in ten-dollar bills that she hopes will make her an attractive target for rape and murder. Shedding her usual demure costume for a bright skirt, too tight across the hips, and a cheap blouse, Grace tries to take a "voyage" to an underclass tabloid world, an alternative environment that she imagines still retains the capacity, however debased, for the emotional intensity necessary for grief.

The motivation of the girls in these stories of imminent rape—"Pastoral Blood," "The Voyage to Rosewood," and the better known "Where Are You Going, Where Have You Been?"—suggests that rape is a complex term in Oates' fiction. More than a violent assault on women, it bears for her uninitiated daughters the ideological trace of authenticity, a crime of "passion" in a sterile culture. It is this promise of experience that fashions the complicity of the Oates daughters, a complicity that leads them to a second stage of consciousness. At the first stage they must recognize their mothers as distinct from themselves. At the second they must make out the cultural construct that they had assumed was personal reflection; they must move through the looking glass to the recognition of their own sexual "identity" as victims. In the tavern when the men at the bar fail to afford her paternal protection and turn her away, Marsha realizes: "I have an identity the men all recognize. It is a struggle for me to understand" (250).

The diction of the title intimates that Marsha's realization is the object of a "voyage" of discovery. Similarly, Oates refers in her film commentary to Connie's "crossing over" (B1). It is this emphasis on the young woman's journey toward expansion of consciousness that may account for the oddly positive tone that prevails in the ending of "Where Are You Going, Where Have You Been?" despite Connie's probable rape and murder:

"My sweet little-blue-eyed girl," he said in a half-sung sigh that had nothing to do with her brown eyes but was taken up just the same by the vast sunlit reaches of the land behind him on all sides of him—so much land that Connie had never seen before and did not recognize except to know that she was going to it. (45–46)

In *The Necessary Blankness: Women in Major American Fiction of the Sixties*, Mary Inez Allen concludes that "no one is better at showing the female consciousness aware of the possibility of rape than Joyce Carol Oates" (151). In the Bildungsroman of Oates' daughters the focus of this content—the threat of rape—may not merely be to express consciousness of rape but to present "rape" as the induction to consciousness. "Violence can't be singled out from an ordinary day!" Jules Wendall of *them* proclaims in the aftermath of the Detroit riots of 1967. "Everyone must live through it again and again. . . . The rapist and his victim rise up from the rubble, eventually, at dawn, and brush themselves off and go down the street to a diner" (473–74).

Elizabeth Dalton condemned in Oates' early works "the violence" that is "mainly violence in the head" (77). But this is precisely where Oates intended to put it. Rape in her works is, however viscerally evoked, exactly what it is in Jules' speech, a symbol of the larger world, and the daughter's place within it, as "ordinary" as the experience of their mothers' kitchens. It is the special burden of Oates' daughters first to recognize this ordinary condition and then find some way to come to terms with it. The novels *them* and *Childwold* present two formal definitions of those terms in contrasting genres—the apocalyptic and the pastoral.

THE APOCALYPTIC CITY

In the prototypical Oates family we are deducing from her domestic fiction, the fall of the father resulting in the inadequacy of his power dangerously exposes the daughter whose gender identity restricts her to powerlessness. The momentary madness of the rapacious father in "Upon the Sweeping Flood" signals this circumstance. But whereas the girls in the consciousness-of-rape stories encountered a specific threatening man, in *them* the whole society is menacing. Although Maureen Wendall, the terrified daughter of this novel, is not raped, her experience of her environment characteristically emphasizes its violence and her weakness in frightening sexualized images or events. Jules Wendall's cosmic rape imagery is appropriate to Oates' expanded presentation of this theme; in *them* the city of Detroit is the rapist and Maureen is the victim. Maureen's consciousness emerges as awareness of this condition and develops as an attempt to deal with it.

In "Imaginary Cities: America," Oates contends that the city must be understood as "a species of hell" (9). Her first novel *With Shuddering Fall* includes a race riot; *them* further develops this theme: the Detroit race riots of 1967 typify the hellish conditions of the contemporary American city as a fiery Armageddon. Oates' use of this religious symbolism, according to Margaret Schaeffer Maney, relates *them* to Nathanael West's *The Day of the Locust*, Ralph Ellison's *Invisible Man*, Hubert Selby's *Last Exit to Brooklyn*, Bernard Malmud's *The Tenants*, and Walker Percy's *Love in the Ruins*, all novels that participate in the contemporary American genre of "the urban apocalypse." Modern cities like Oates' Detroit, Maney argues, are fraught with "postmodern analogues to the Great Tribulation" of the biblical Revelations: "perverted materialism . . . , the racially divided city, the death of love, endemic violence, and . . . the dissociation of being" (211). Maureen Wendall, especially, registers each of these contemporary tribulations in her own person.

First, she experiences the prevalent racial tension of Detroit as personal threat that interferes with her own needs. This is apparent in the scene where she witnesses a knife fight from the window of a bus and is too frightened to disembark to attend class. But this paralyzing fear that she associates with "Negroes" in this instance is embedded within a generalized sexual threat Maureen believes that she must overcome in order to survive. She determines that nothing will prevent her from getting an education:

not the men cruising the neighborhood in low-slung flashy cars, white or Negro men leaning out car windows asking her if she'd like a ride, not the policemen in squad cars eying her, not the dirty drab old men riding the city buses perpetually, staring at her.(385)

This pervasive atmosphere of violence and sexual threat, of which racial tension is but one metaphor, culminates in the novel in events of both social and personal apocalypse—the Detroit race riot and Maureen's beating and resultant mental breakdown.

Out of her intuition of "perverted materialism," the second tribulation typical of the apocalyptic city, seventeen-year-old Maureen becomes a prostitute in order to acquire money, which, even when she is a child, she understands as the secret value at the center of family life: "anything might be shouted out that had to do with people, but nothing about money—the facts of money—could be mentioned out loud" (127).

Maureen's fantasies about payment for intercourse demystify the meaning of money. The money she receives from men, "magical" and "secret from all the world," is of central importance because it provides her with what her constant fearfulness demonstrates she sorely lacks: "Its power would become hers" (191). Dressed in her school uniform, little Maureen hustles older men, the weak daughter prostituting herself to procure something of the power of the fathers. Her step-father's discovery of her secret cache provokes the brutal beating that severely damages Maureen's body, but, more important, also destroys her dearly purchased false security and provokes her mental collapse, an extreme experience of "dissociation of being," the third apocalyptic precondition.

"[M]y mind gave up," Maureen confides in a letter to "Miss Oates," (312) who was once her teacher. "The profound disorganization of mind, personality or behavior that results in an individual's inability to tolerate the demands of the social environment," Otto Friedrich's definition of psychosis (8), describes Maureen's condition. Her mother's appraisal is, however, more succint and more germane: "A woman grows up to take all the shit she can from men, then she breaks down, that's the way it is" (207). Maureen, ill, "asleep in her body," dreams in fragments the sexual episodes of her past; "What does it mean to be a woman?" she wonders (300). When finally she begins to recover, to awaken to the events around her, "she is afraid," and characteristically she experiences her fear as the threat of sexual violation: "She feels open, as if her legs have been yanked apart, anything can happen" (308).

Phyllis Chesler argues in *Women and Madness* that insanity is a problem of gender: "What we consider 'madness,' whether it appears in women or men, is either the acting out of the devalued female role or the total or partial rejection of one's sex-role-stereotype" (56). Maureen's madness represents both the frightening recognition of gender constraint and the simultaneous necessity to escape its imposition; although in Oates' narratives of female development, it is the recognition that somewhat uneasily triumphs.

Psychological ordeal in Oates' works is the mark of her characters' experience of actuality in the absence of their ability to conceptualize reality, the vast social and economic forces that determine them. In her review of *The Dollmaker*, set like *them* in Detroit, Oates describes that city as typifying "the complex economic knot of modern industrial society" ("Joyce Carol Oates on Harriet Arnow's *The Dollmaker*" 608). And, in fact, Maureen's perception of actual sexual threat is a symptom of her family's real economic plight, a process of symbolic conversion that is also evident in her adolescent foray into prostitution and her later goal of a secure marriage, both projects in which economic motivation is restricted to sexual expression. Oates' narratives of the daughters' insanity must, therefore, be read as social criticism. Thus, the recoveries of her young madwomen are not cures that indicate their succesful adaptation to a healthy society but evidence of their courageous progress toward consciousness of the limitations of their general condition.

The brutality Maureen experiences in her own family provides a personal instance of the "endemic violence" of Detroit, the fourth and last "tribulation" she recognizes as a general situation by reading a year's worth of newspapers after her thirteen-month illness. As she examines old newspapers trying to recapture the year she has lost, Maureen is terrified to recognize the endless cycle of violence revealed by the headlines: "In the library I started sweating, so afraid. How can I live my life if the world is like this? The world can't be lived, no one can live it right" (310).

Since family care and money have failed her, all that Maureen has to pit against her realization of personal and public disorder is consciousness, a quality she is eager to develop throughout the novel in her enthusiasm for the library as a child, her determination to attend class as an adult, and even in her decision to marry her night-school teacher. During her childhood the library was a place of refuge, a precious and delicate intermission in chaotic family life, and what Maureeen attempted to borrow along with the children's books that she read in the strictly prescribed sequence of their placement on the Young People's shelf was the imposition of a magical order. But after her illness, a more genuine sense of the operation of consciousness emerges. In letters written from the library to her famous teacher,[8] Maureen rejects such magical control, seeking through knowledge more practical approaches to life as she has experienced it: "I want to learn whatever I can, maybe it will help me not to be afraid" (310). But she contrasts the kind of classic literature "Miss Oates" taught in the night class to her own life and rejects the literature: "none of those books are worth anything. . . . Those things didn't happen. . . . In my life something happened and I have to keep thinking of it, over and over" (313).

Maureen's experience, chaotic and urgent, eludes her attempts at the imposition of conceptual order. This is the meaning of Maureen's lost homeroom secretary's notebook, which Oates said in an interview was "really the worst thing that happened to her in the whole novel."[9] The notebook contained all the records of Room 202 since 1953, and young Maureen was deeply honored at being given the responsibility of carefully recording weekly minutes in "difficult to erase dark-blue ink" (152). When she accidentally lost the book on her way home from school, Maureen was so upset she felt "that her mind was becoming undone" (158).

The lesson Maureen learned painfully as a child—that order can be destroyed—is confirmed by her brutal adolescent experience. "What is form?" she demands in her letters to Miss Oates. "Why is it better than the way life happens by itself?" (318). Maureen's own written style is formless, a style Jim Randolph, the composition teacher whom she marries, characterizes as insane, but it is an "insanity he had been drawn to; and yet it was not insanity, not really. He understood her words as they passed through him, easily" (409).

It is the direct intensity of Maureen's perception—fearful, attractive, repulsive, and familiar, a style of consciousness that registers the threat of the city—that touches Jim. It is precisely this courage to conceptualize overwhelming experience that distinguishes Maureen from her mother whom she thinks of as submerged in dreamy "junk": "she seems wide awake, she's always going somewhere and she's always ready for a laugh, but really her life is all asleep" (409).

In "Swamps" and *With Shuddering Fall*, the presence of "junk" indicates an inundation by culture that signals disorder. It is important to observe that Maureen Wendall, demonstrably the most victimized daughter of Oates' novels, whom Oates herself describes as "passive" ("An Interview with Joyce Carol Oates" 5), defines herself, in contrast to her mother, as actively and consciously resisting this detrimental influx and as awakened after the sleep of her mental breakdown.

Maureen's rape of consciousness—her recognition of the violence endemic in her culture—marks the difference between the maturing daughters and the childish mothers of Oates' domestic fiction:

She couldn't be like her mother, always ready for the next day, always curious . . . ready to begin all over again. She was not her mother's daughter. She felt an almost physical revulsion for that kind of woman, Loretta's kind, their hair in curlers and their monkeyish faces set for a good laugh. (387)

Although Loretta provides care and nurturance during Maureen's long illness, she deserves the revulsion Maureen expresses here. Slovenly, she has taken advantage of Maureen's compulsive neatness to use her as a servant; self-indulgent, Loretta has unconsciously instigated, out of her own laziness, the veiled sexual relationship between Maureen and her step-father that reaches its perverse climax in the beating. Yet Maureen's strategic consciousness comes at a price; rejecting her mother's sloppy character—the failure to understand and protect her daughter from the conditions of their mutual insecurity—Maureen must, she believes, also reject her mother's optimism and occasional passion.

In the economic and sexual ghetto occupied by the Wendall women, Maureen has been unable to secure safety through family nurture, money, or intellectual "form." Urgently restricted by all the threatening vitality of Oates' violent city, Maureen can imagine only one order that seems to include all the conditions of actual living and the possibility of security: marriage. "I want to marry a man and fall in love and be protected by him" (312), Maureen confides. "Tomorrow night I'll see the man I have picked out to love. . . . I want him to marry me. I am going to make this happen and begin my life" (315–316).

At Maureen's stage of development toward autonomy, Oates' daughters are not conditioned by their mothers, but despite differences in awareness, they are still conditioned like them. Yet unlike Loretta who drifts into relationships, Maureen consciously plots a marriage as her only option for self-protection. But this option is not a solution, as Jules warns in a concluding speech that returns to the rape-of-consciousness motif that informs this apocalyptic novel:

don't forget that this place here can burn down too. Men can come back in your life, Maureen, they can beat you up again and force your knees apart, why not? There's so much of it in the world, so much semen, so many men! Can't it happen? Won't it happen? Wouldn't you really want it to happen? (478)

THE PASTORAL DAUGHTER

Whereas the apocalyptic novel *them* presents the actuality of the gendered powerlessness of women, *Childwold* is a pastoral dream of the creation of an empowered woman. Just as Maureen Wendall is the most conspicuous register of the apocalyptic city in *them*, Laney Bartlett is the most conspicuous representative of the pastoral project in *Childwold*. Unlike Maureen, whose menstrual blood evokes associations of the fatality that infects Detroit,[10] the arrival of Laney's first period reminds her of the return from anemia to health, the "blood a blessing" (193). Refusing the solicitude of a sickbed, she spends the afternoon on horseback becoming conscious of the vitality of the landscape around her:

Alive, alive. Everything is alive. . . . Bankside bushes, sumac and willow, and vines trailing into the creek dry as corn shucks, mustard weed high as your shoulder, flies buzzing, bees everywhere, chicory, witch grass, small white butterflies . . . the hot deep blue sky . . . another of the sacred places you will remember all your life. (195)

In cadence and subject this passage is reminiscent of Whitman's use of catalogues in "Song of Myself":

> a kelson of creation is love,
> And limitless are leaves stiff or drooping in the fields,
> And brown ants in the little wells beneath them,
> And mossy scabs of worm fence, heap'd stones, elder, mullein and poke-
> weed (5.95–98).

In both passages, closely observed details of the natural world find expression as sensual images and words through repeated and regular rhythmic units that celebrate the profusion and possibility of experience.

But the point of view in the novel makes it impossible to simply interpret Laney as the happy opposite of sad Maureen. It is important to note that the fresh and vivid sensuality of the quoted passage is a projection onto the "you" of Laney by the enervated poet-philosopher Fitz John Kasch, who explains in the first line of the novel: "That final year of my life, I often dreamed of Evangeline" (10). In form, the book presents successive images and episodes of Kasch's dreaming. Just as Whitman projects "Walt" as a resurrection of the holy potency of old male gods,[11] in Kasch's projection "Evangeline" reclaims the energetic divinity of the ideal female.

"Pastoral poetry affects the manner or matter of rustic life," G. P. Marsh noted, "not for accurate description, but as a purely artistic device for conveying the interests of the poet himself, of the society not rural in which he lives."[12] In *Childwold* those interests reflect the worldly failures of Fitz John Kasch and his longing for pastoral retreat. In the action of the story, bumbling Kasch escapes from a failed marriage and a university post to Yewville in Oates' Eden County to take up residence in a carriage house behind his childhood home. Mimicking Thoreau, that prototype of the romantic retreat, he describes his return as an effort "to live deliberately, to retreat from history, both personal and collective . . . to drive life into a corner and reduce it to its lowest terms" (21). The alternative is suicide.

"Maniac. Pervert. But lonely," Kasch describes himself. "Where I lived and what I lived for. . . . Find a girl and bring her back to the room" (21). On an evening ramble in this state of mind he encounters fourteen-year-old Laney Bartlett at the center of a drunken crowd of threatening teenage boys. This feisty "Evangeline," who smells of cheap wine, is, Kasch believes, "prematurely aged, dirtied, used, wise" (54), and yet she is also an unformed child whom he befriends in an antic style and upon whom he fixes his fantasies.

In the course of the novel Kasch, attempting to redress the imbalance of his own intellectualized condition, marries his overdeveloped "head" to the fetid "body" of Laney's mother, Arlene. Fitz John, an abstract and abstracted bridegroom, is poorly equipped to survive the violence contingent on Arlene's careless sensuality. Attempting to protect her from the jealous wrath of a former lover, Kasch accidentally kills the assailant, an act that forces him further into insane retirement.

It is from this perspective that Kasch creates the idealization of Evangeline, "mere essence; no human woman at all" (191–192), a more successful realization of the mind/body marriage. In her, Kasch joins the rich texture that he ascribes to female experience to his own style of masculine consciousness, which he shares with Laney in the form of books and wider exposure to culture.

Oates has written that "Nature" is an "Invention of civilization," an "idea" that is the "counterpart of the City," which functions as the "dramatic backdrop against which fictional persons enact their representative struggles with those values the city embodies" ("Imaginary Cities" 10). Laney, then, the child of Nature, must be viewed as a pastoral symbol of reparation. As we observed in the threatening animation of Detroit, raw energy is not enough. Maureen tries without success to combine vitality with order through consciousness. But Kasch's Laney is the positive expression of the potential for such combination.

Arlene Bartlett, Laney's mother, the earth goddess gone to seed, is characterized not by the healthful profusion of nature but by the confusion of her ramshackle house when a welfare worker arrives for an unexpected investigation: The kitchen is a sight, the boys' room smells of urine, and the stairway is littered with discarded shoes, toys, "towels, used Kleenex, crusts from that morning's toast" (205).

But unlike her mother's house, Laney's attic bedroom can balance both profusion and order. The room contains a rich mixture of colors, textures, and objects that combine to form a coherent design: "There were floral designs and stripes and patches of color, like the pieces of a jigsaw puzzle." To her mother, Laney's room exhibits unfathomable meaning and surprising comfort: "it reminded her of photographs in glossy magazines, where rooms were displayed because they meant something" (90). Arlene longs to curl up under the colorful quilts with her daughter, and it is with great relief that she leads the welfare investigator "up to Laney's room, the one neat room in the house, bed made and things in order . . . " (206).

Whereas Loretta Wendall usually disregards her daughter's separateness, Arlene Bartlett observes and respects the special and singular identity of which Laney's distinctive bedroom is an emblem: "Well it *was* a kingdom," Arlene muses, "Laney's own, and nothing in the house could compare" (92). Like Maureen and Loretta, however, Laney is distinguished from her mother by the quality of the daughter's consciousness. But unlike the timid and fearful Maureen, Laney's scrappy courage and her relationship to Kasch allow her to develop that consciousness beyond a mode of self-protection into a means of growth. Laney's capacity for growth as a characteristic of consciousness is distinguished from that of her mother in parallel but opposing reactions during separate visits to museums.

Arlene discovers at the museum a renewed contentment in her own contraction. Transfixed by a large map of Eden County, she runs her finger across the configurations of her own area until she locates the tiny village of Childwold: "she'd been born and lived all her life . . . within a few inches on this map. . . . I've been happy here, she thought" (218). In contrast to the mother's delight in the contraction of her own experience, the daughter feels the excitement of expansion. An exhibition of photographs of the landscape and people of her own region has for Laney the quality of epiphany: "Sunrise . . . mountains . . . the blossoming of light in leaves...you want to cry out in amazement that you have never seen anything before" (144–145). In contrast to her mother's contentment in restriction, Laney's experience of a new order of consciousness—art—enlarges her, opens her to new possibility.

Both genres, the apocalyptic and the pastoral, founded on consciousness of societal failure, are utopian propositions about the fallen world. Out of the ashes of the devastated city, better forms may yet emerge. In the simplified and isolated retreat of the bucolic idyll something sustaining may be imagined. The endings of both *them* and *Childwold*, however, stress ambiguity rather than possibility. Jules' last speech raises important questions: If "rape" is the general condition of humanity, can Maureen ever be safe? And if "rape" is the metaphor for the growth of consciousness, would she really want to be?

Laney's energetic self-defense, which attracts Kasch at the beginning of *Childwold*, suggests that at fourteen she comprehends and can cope with general conditions of brutality that Maureen struggles well into young womanhood to come to terms with. In the female developmental model this chapter proposes, *Childwold* advances from the rape of consciousness to the possibility of the growth of consciousness beyond the perception of victimization. Yet, although the last words of the novel are Laney's, they hint not at her advancement but at her limitation as Kasch's pastoral projection. Echoing the query of her grandfather before his death, Laney demands, "A sign, a sign . . . ?" (287). Yet just as neither God nor the universe replied to old Joseph, Laney's creator, Fitz John Kasch, huddled in the deteriorating abandoned Bartlett home, maintains his silence. This ambiguous ending implies that Laney's very existence is dependent on Kasch's imagination, that she is largely a creature of his language in the novel, and that her positive ability to balance profusion and order is possible because of Kasch's withdrawal from social constraint into the transgressive freedom of insanity. At this point the possibility of total human capacity rather than ideological limitation remains a pastoral dream.

In spite of the qualification of this ending, however, Oates observed in 1980 that *Childwold*, published in 1977, is "meant to point beyond its narrative conclusion to a 'future' beyond the closing paragraph. (That is, Laney's 'future' as an independent and even educated young woman—free of Kasch's imagination)" ("Speaking about Short Fiction" 243). That Oates' optimism must find expression exterior to the novel reinforces what the use of the pastoral convention in *Childwold* implies: the subtlety and strength of gender restriction in any but idealized circumstances. It is not until a more recent novel that Oates addresses the possibility of total female experience within the text itself. In *Marya*, which we shall consider in another chapter as a summary of family themes, Oates expresses the possibility of female development of consciousness beyond the confines of male imagination.

THE FACTS OF LIFE

We have traced sequential stages in the development of Oates' daughters: the recognition of the self as distinct from the mother, the mirror-gaze of complex identity, the rape of consciousness and the consciousness of rape, and the consciousness of possibility. The consistent theme throughout is the growth of perception and the concomitant refusal of the traditional innocence of the young woman.

In *them* and *Childwold* both Maureen and Laney deliberate about the theme of knowledge. Just as Maureen complains of Miss Oates' literature, which omits actual experience, Laney also criticizes a literary genre that obscures pertinent information. Laney reads the most degenerate form of the female fiction McNall defined as "romantic"—her mother's tabloid papers and magazines with stories like "God Sent Me a Defective Baby." But, as Laney observes, the magazine stories "spoke to you but they lied" (215) because

if there were money problems or unemployment or strikes or an inflated economy
the girls in the magazines knew nothing of such things, they were to blame, there
was no larger world, *they* were sinful and selfish and cruel and ignorant, the very
center of the universe lay between their legs. (214)

In the nineteenth century William Dean Howells campaigned for a
literature that "could be openly spoken of before the tenderest society bud
at dinner," stories "chaste" enough to spare an audience of "ladies" and
"young girls" the sordid details of sexuality.[13] But in Oates' twentieth
century, Laney's reading suggests that the innocence of women is maintained by confining them to the sordid details of sex through suppression
of the genuine "facts of life." For, as Maureen discovered, money is the
secret women learn at their peril.

The division of power and nurturance as the basis for Oates' family
structure confines her mothers to the facts of sex, and in the ideological
model they try to evade, daughters are expected to conform to the same
paradoxical "innocence." McNall insists that the fusion of female roles
effected by the close connection of mothers and daughters reinforces a
destructive chain of women's economic dependence: the ideology of such
dependency "draws much of its strength from the female child's special
experience of dependence on the mother" (3).

Oates' developmental themes of recognition and consciousness chart
the daughters' rejection of dependence on the mothers to effect the fission
of female family roles. In Oates' family fiction, mothers like Loretta and
Arlene—whom critics describe as active, canny, cat-like, and agile—are
true innocents. Too ignorant to seek any knowledge of forces operating
beyond the confines of their bodies, they are restricted to sex roles,
survivors, not shapers, of their own destinies. The so-called passive young
women in Oates' novels, by contrast, insistently refuse the traditional
innocence of daughters by fully experiencing rapacious society and then
attempting to come to terms with it. Even in the apocalyptic novel, which
presents conditions at their worst, where the daughter must, she believes,
accept her restriction to sex role as a means of self-protection, her choice
is conscious rather than naive; and inspired by the pastoral project of
Childwold, Oates predicts an autonomous future for Laney Bartlett. Consciously exploiting rather than merely accepting their sexuality, Oates'
daughters refuse their mothers' unwitting acquiescence by forging connections to suburban husbands, demon-lovers, and mentor-fathers with
whom they seek to enter unknown worlds of knowledge, money, and force
beyond their mothers' ghetto walls.

Chapter Three

Brothers and Sisters: The Refusal of Substitute Relation

Joyce Carol Oates' brothers and sisters lead lives emotionally connected but inevitably separated by gender. Through parallel treatments of the brother and the sister, Oates deals with the issues of masculine power as well as feminine powerlessness. The narratives of Maureen Wendall of *them* and Laney Bartlett of *Childwold* in Chapter 2 provide the outline of the story of the sister. In this chapter, we shall develop the story of the brother with special reference to Jules Wendall of *them*. We shall also consider the parallel treatment of a brother and sister in *Angel of Light*. The relationship of the brother and sister, like that of the mother and daughter, demonstrates the refusal of regressive innocence. Oates' siblings must finally relinquish their comforting childhood bond and part to confront separate issues of adult empowerment.

As we have observed, Oates' stories of adolescent daughters question the stereotype of the "romantic" heroine. Similarly, her stories of teenage sons interrogate generic concepts of the hero. In *them* and *Angel of Light* Oates considers the relevance of conventional presentations of the comic and the tragic hero to the contemporary young man's violent predicament.

INDUCTION INTO VIOLENCE

Kess in the early short story "A Legacy" provides a striking instance of the brother's problem in Oates' family fiction. For his sister Laura, Kess has only one identity: he is the fascinating older brother. His irrepressible high spirits may have caused her to break her leg in a childhood accident, but what she remembers of the incident is how he entertained her afterward by flinging himself over the creek on a rope swing in "terrific flight" and by dangling an old hen in front of her by the wings so she could watch it dance (*By the North Gate* 176). Her image of that lively thirteen-year-old boy bears little resemblance to the apathetic man she is brought to visit. Kess is awaiting execution for murder, and Laura has come to say good-bye.

In prison Kess has begun to smoke, a habit that symbolizes his sense of personal dissolution. He has come to enjoy smoking, he explains, because "It wears things out inside," so that when the day comes for his execution there "won't be nothin' left...for them to do it to" (174). Something from beyond the self that penetrates the deepest recesses of his being, the cigarette that burns away his essence to leave only the "outside" shell is the "legacy" Kess passes to Laura through the bars of his cell. It is also the emblem of his ideological transformation. Kess has imbibed violence the way he has inhaled smoke, to dissolve his essential character. He has taken violence into himself, and it has destroyed him.

The difference between the sister and brother in Oates' fiction may be understood in their varying responses to violence. The sister may be penetrated in the act of rape by the endemic violence of her social situation, but rarely does she herself become violent. In fact, female violence in Oates' works is always the mark of transgression, the attempt to resist determinant conditions. But brutalized by experience, the brother joins the practice of violence. The destructive aggression of the adult male world penetrates Kess like the smoke he willingly drags into his lungs, and he is corrupted by it.

The transfiguration from the lively brother to the ruined young male sketched in this story is more fully developed in the portrayal of Vale, Laney Bartlett's older brother in *Childwold*. Like Kess, Vale has taken violence into himself; having tasted blood (250) in the war in Vietnam, he has changed from an unruly kid to a brutal young man. Like Laura, Laney remembers the protective strength of an older brother, and like Laura, she does not recognize her brother after his transformation through violence:

They killed him . . . he disappeared, someone else was shipped back, Vale died, Vale had been smashed, his face wasn't put together right . . . it wasn't Vale, Vale died, was sent away in a gigantic jet plane and never came back. (34–35)

Irreparably damaged psychically as well as physically, during the novel Vale dispassionately murders at least two people.

Although Kess in the early story is only damaged "inside," Vale, externally scarred and morally psychopathic, is devastated both inside and out. The escalation of destruction in the later novel is the result of Oates' insertion of Vale's violence into a generalized social context. His presence is the ironic foil to the idealization of "Evangeline." His name, like hers, evokes pastoral tradition, but bucolic "Vale" is presented not, like Laney, in images of idyllic retreat but in the antithetical imagery of degraded community: "Lone-Lee's Take-Out, barbed wire fences . . . No Trespassing, concrete. . . . What is this place, Vale asked, I don't know this place, who are these people?" (250).

Kess's story shows that male adolescence is the induction into violence; Vale's experience demonstrates that the impetus to that induction is a destructive society. Whereas the sister in Oates' fiction must struggle to obtain knowledge of the power that operates on rather than through her in order to ensure both her survival and her development, the brother acquires the problematic power of the adult male world. He must struggle to become its agent without being destroyed by it.

THE BROTHER'S COMEDY

The "typical hero of romance," writes Northrop Frye, "whose actions are marvelous but who is identified as a human being" is the protagonist of the legend or folk tale (33). According to Bruno Bettelheim the purpose of this genre is to embody through the adventure of the hero the reassurance "that a struggle against severe difficulties in life . . . is an intrinsic part of human existence—but that if one . . . steadfastly meets unexpected and unjust hardships, one masters all obstacles and . . . emerges victorious" (8). Bettelheim also contends that the tale encourages moral development by counseling that to "find deeper meaning, one must become able to transcend the narrow confines of self-centered existence" (3–4). Through Jules Wendall of *them* Oates tests the feasibility of the beneficent empowerment of the traditional romantic hero in modern life.

Jules' story contains classic elements of the folk tale as outlined by Vladimir Propp.[1] First, a "lack" is discerned that sets in motion a quest to eliminate it. During his adventure, the hero meets one or more "donors" who provide useful orientation on the accomplishment of this objective. He then proceeds to a location where the reparation may be accomplished and engages in a victorious struggle with the "villain" of the tale, who has been previously introduced. Finally, the hero returns to his community, where his achievement is rewarded by his marriage to the princess and his ascension to the throne.

The lack that Jules is sensitive enough to discern is his family's deficient power. He is particulary aware of his father's ineffectual submissiveness:

He tried to think of his father as a soldier, but he kept seeing a slack-bellied man in the front room drinking beer, waiting. What had his father been waiting for? His father hadn't even played with the deck of cards, as Loretta and Jules did. What was being played out for him, which cards were being turned over, he hadn't even interest to find out—it was being done for him, no matter. And so his father had waited. (66)

Acutely conscious of his family's pervasive helplessness, young Jules intuits his destiny: "*Someday I will change all this*, he thought with a flash of joy" (93).

In the traditional folk story the donor is the figure who, after recognizing the hero's merit, grants him some magical boon that aids him in his quest. The characters in *them* who perform this function are Faye, the silver-blond mistress of a very wealthy man, and Bernard Geffen, a would-be hoodlum.

One afternoon while he is crossing a busy Detroit street, Jules is almost run over by a speeding car. Still reeling from this near-miss, he is then jostled roughly by a passing pedestrian. Faye, a beautiful stranger who has witnessed these events, summons a cab and takes Jules back to her apartment to make him her lover. Described as "a northern . . . fairy-tale princess . . . cold, enchanting" (224), Faye represents freedom from commitment to other people. But just as the recognition of Jules' worthiness is not, in this instance, based on the hero's excellence, the value of the magic knowledge the donor imparts is also questionable. As a result of his relationship with Faye, Jules discovers that

His freedom was important. . . . Every thought dragged him back to that mess of a family but technically he was free. "I think that if I could get enough money to fix them all up," he told Faye, "to get some good doctor for my sister, then . . . I guess I'd take off for California and see what's out there." "There's nothing out there," Faye said, yawning. (220)

If Faye's ennui here raises doubts about the value of personal independence for the American hero, Jules' experience of Bernard Geffen disputes the value of what the second donor appears to promise: the American "adventure" (223) of financial success. Whereas Faye is coolly detached, Bernard with his flurry of checks, his conversation about yachts (222) and "connections" (227) is wildly manic. He is a speeded-up combination of Cody and Wolfsheim to Jules' Jimmy Gatz.[2] The three days Jules is in his employ are crammed with fast cars, fast talk, fast deals: "Drive straight ahead," Bernard orders, "I want to think. I have to plan the rest of my life this morning," and Jules learns from Geffen's example that he, too, may have the fabulous ability to "make nearly anything happen" (227). Bernard embodies for Jules all the money-driven possibility of the American dream, but his violent death—"his throat freshly slit and the butcher knife placed in his hand" (245)—reveals the American nightmare. With $10,000 Bernard had issued him for the purchase of a new Cadillac in hand, Jules feels as if he "had become immortal" (238), but the shocking realization of mortality, "the rumpled, soft, filthy feel of bills," dominates as Jules, terror-stricken at the sight of Bernard's blood, hastily stuffs the wads of money into the pockets of his murdered employer's coat (245).

Like every traditional questing hero, Jules seeks a site where reparation is possible. His journey takes him through the legendary Southwest as far as Texas, but his "faith in the future" and an "ideal landscape," a "wilderness," (276) is tested by the actual scenery: "Beaumont, Texas. No mountains, no beauty. . . . The spread of land from Detroit to Beaumont was similar in the cities and the country" (284). As he and his girlfriend Nadine drive down a road that winds past oil refineries and tar-paper shanties to end up at the city dump, her comment summarizes their disappointed reaction: "This is a place to die in" (285). In contradiction to Propp's pattern, Jules must go home to Detroit to finally confront the villain of the piece.

Before he was sixteen years old, Jules had been accosted by a policeman who put his pistol to the boy's temple and pulled the trigger. Finding the clip empty, the cop cracked the gun butt across Jules' skull, and, stooping to lift Jules' wallet, left him unconscious in a vacant building. Significantly, Jules' vicious father, Howard Wendall, had been a cop. The police in *them* are not stalwart representatives of social order; they stand, instead, for violent paternal abuse of power as the definitive condition of urban life. Deadly obstacles to Jules' hopes to realize his heroic potential, the police are the villainous dragons of this tale. And when Jules is caught up in the Detroit riot that serves as the climax of the novel, he finds himself once again in an empty building with a brutal policeman. But this time it is Jules who pulls the trigger and murders the cop.

In the denouement that follows this questionable conquest, Jules tastes the traditional reward of the fairy-tale hero. The community honors him: in the aftermath of the riot Jules appears on television as an authority who is able to interpret the destructive turmoil, and, funded by a federal poverty grant, he sets off once again, with renewed optimism, to seek his fortune, in California, the one "wilderness" he has yet to use up. He even plans to find and wed Nadine Greene, the elusive princess of the story.

How is the reader to interpret Jules' action? Is he to be understood as the reassurring example of perseverance and mastery of Bettelheim's first formulation? Must we read his capitulation to the violence that surrounds him as heroic achievement? The answer to this question is evidently ambiguous. Not only has Jules' story generated "a surprising range of critical reaction," according to Linda Wagner (xxv),[3] but provoked by what she perceived as gross misreadings of *them* in reviews of the novel, Oates herself defended Jules against "well-educated, liberal, handsomely-paid New York" critics too insulated from "poverty in America" to appreciate the "marvelous" accomplishment of "my young hero" ("Transformations of Self" 57–58). But although Oates declared that the novel's conclusion hints that Jules is "on his way to some sort of American success," she qualified that assertion: "In *Them*, I saw Jules as a kind of American success in an ironic sense, of course. He is a hero and a murderer at once. I think that is ironic. I hope it is" ("An Interview with Joyce Carol Oates" 308).

The irony Oates claims is supported by her satiric treatment of the generic requirements of the romance. Jules, an energetic brother figure, is physically and morally equipped to be a hero. He desperately wants to be a hero; he valiantly tries to be a hero; but each of the narrative criteria of heroism is undercut by the conditions of the world in which his story is told. The evidence of his superior worth is dubious; the donors are defective; the land of promise disappointing; and the moral victory of good over evil in the climactic battle between the hero and villain remains uncertain at best.

Despite his author's editorial support, even Jules understands his act of murder as moral capitulation. He has spent his childhood in a successful attempt to evade the petty but violent rage that characterizes his father, Howard Wendall. And, on the occasion of Howard's death, Jules observes his own special triumph:

Jules felt a flash of satisfaction, almost of joy. No, he hadn't killed his father. His own anger had been kept back for years, kept successfully back; he hadn't hurt anyone. . . . He felt that his father's essence, that muttering dark anger, had surrounded him and almost penetrated him, but had not quite penetrated him; he was free. (135–136)

Like Kess and Vale in our previous examples, Jules is endowed with the talent, charm, energy, and high spirits that mark him from youth as a hero rather than a murderer. Unlike them, however, he recognizes and seeks to avoid the pervasive violence of the adult male, yet like both of these young men he becomes a killer in spite of his struggle to evade this fate. "My God, give me a chance," Jules yells to the ruthless policeman whom he finally kills; "Let me out of the back door, will you?" (467). But these stories intimate no way out for the poor young man in American society. Trying to escape, Jules smashes the policeman in the face and feels "the gristle of the man's nose breaking....Having done this, he had done everything. It was over. His blood ran wild, he was not to blame for anything, why should he stop? He aimed the rifle into the man's face and pulled the trigger" (468).

What is the nature of this wild border all three of these youthful protagonists have crossed? To answer this question we must consider the inception of Jules' story in a "lack" of power. In *Power and Innocence: A Search for the Sources of Violence*, Rollo May describes the struggle for power as a natural assertion of significance that may escalate to its extreme form of violence when all other means have been thwarted (21). The brothers in Oates' working class families illustrate the positive impulse to achieve personal agency. But the fathers exhibit the frustration of that impulse, which results in violence. As we have observed, economic circumstance renders the fathers' strategies of empowerment ineffectual and frustrating. The result is a personal, familial, and social life marked by violent expressions of the maladaptive "anger" Jules describes as the principal characteristic of Howard Wendall:

Yes, anger was at the core of him; his soul was anger, made up of anger. Anger for what? For nothing, for himself, for life, for the assembly line, for the cockroaches, for the dripping toilet. . . . Anger. No money. Where had the money gone? Where would the money come from? Anger, money. His father. (135)

Anger, money, father. These are the terms that mark the boundaries of the brother's territory in Oates' fiction. The dangerous region entered by the boys in her works is the adult world of American capitalism, a competitive arena in which the working-class fathers inevitably lose. Nevertheless, young Jules Wendall imagines his special destiny in images of financial success: "He felt his true essence was of great value and would someday be expressed in ordinary signs of cars and women" (110). His story, however, disputes the ideological basis for such dreams.

Constance Rourke has suggested the gradual evolution of an American comic archetype born out of the tales of the sharp-dealing Yankee peddler and the combative frontiersman.[4] Oates' contemporary version of the folk hero is bred as well out of the romantic lover and the movie gangster. Ambitious Jules attempts to emulate all of these heroes, but nothing in this mythical heritage is adequate to his quest for fulfillment. An American picaro, he roams the Southwest, but he cannot overcome its obstacles. His letters home recount only his professional failures. Real estate swindler, willing victim of bizarre government medical experiments, odd-job man, legal car thief—Jules does not find his fortune in the golden West; nor does he manage to secure the golden girl: Nadine Greene, the Zelda to his Scott, the Daisy to his Gatsby, blasts him with a pistol to end their disappointing affair. And the contest of wills, which should signal the hero's victory over adversity, marks Jules' decline into depravity.

Parody, Oates explains, is "the playing of forms out of which life has disappeared" (*The Edge of Impossibility* 11). And through Jules' story, *them* presents an elaborate parody of the forms of American heroics—independence, aggression, and greed—that promote economic competition as indispensable for positive achievement. The multiple caricatures that contribute to Jules' story cooperate in an elaborate critique of the quintessential American hero defined by R.W.B. Lewis as the American Adam: "a hero of a new adventure: an individual emancipated from history, happily bereft of ancestry, untouched and undefiled by the usual inheritances of family and race; an individual standing alone, self-reliant and self-propelling, ready to confront whatever awaited" (5).

Although the qualities of isolation, confrontation, and self-aggrandizement may have admirably served the gallery of Adamic precursors *them* satirizes, they miserably fail Jules Wendall. In an essay entitled "The Death Throes of Romanticism," Oates explains why:

Where at one point in civilization, this very masculine, combative ideal of an "I" set against all other "I's"—and against nature as well—was necessary in order to wrench man from hermetic contemplation of a God-centered universe and get him into action, it is no longer necessary, its health has become a pathology, and whoever clings to its outmoded concepts will die. (115)

Jules' legitimate claim to heroism rests not on his persistence in the old mode of pernicious competition, which has conditioned the failed fathers of Oates' oeuvre, but on his tentative advancement into a new mode of social cooperation. For Bettelheim, we recall, the ultimate achievement of the folk hero is the movement away from "self-centered existence" toward communal contribution. "Emancipated from history" and "untouched and undefiled" by "family," while trying to fulfill his destiny as an American hero, Jules discovers he is too much alone. "*I have come to the conclusion,*"

Jules writes Loretta and Maureen from Dallas, *"that people are all lonely, each one of us"* (295–296). It has been his *"main discovery"* he adds from Tulsa, that *"the Spirit of the Lord in us all . . . makes us able to talk to one another and love one another"* (306).

In these statements Jules shifts from the concern for personal power sought by the romantic hero Oates considers maladaptive to the kind of productive power Rollo May classifies as *nutrient*: power *for* rather than *against* the other (109). As she observed to Dale Boesky:

In *them* I deal in utter seriousness with the possibility of the transformation of our culture by eastern religion—at least the 'mysticism' of the Indian saint who teaches, contrary to what America teaches Maureen and Jules, that 'we are all members of a single family.' ("Correspondence with Miss Joyce Carol Oates" 484)

In this interpretative postscript, reminiscent of her afterthoughts on Laney Bartlett's rosy future, Oates suggests something like the sanctification of Jules Wendall, the murderer/hero of her much more ambivalent novel, an indication, I believe, that in Jules' narrative Oates reaches the ideological limits that her works struggle to redefine.

Joyce Carol Oates' parodic fiction discloses what is deleterious and anachronistic in the ideological presuppositions shaping American culture. As Jules' story indicates, the utopian project of such works is not to reject power as such but to bring it back into ideal conjunction with nurturance. We may recognize in Jules Wendall's comedy of violence and love, then, the unsuccessful but revelatory effort to solve the initial contradiction impelling all of Oates' literary production, and we will observe in the parody of tragedy that structures *Angel of Light* a related effort to transmute social violence into a means of communal rehabilitation.

THE FAMILY TRAGEDY

Angel of Light is a modern-dress *Oresteia*.[5] Oates' renovated cast of characters includes Maurie Halleck, a depressed government prosecutor, as Agamemmnon and his elegant and unfaithful wife Isabel de Benavente Halleck as Clytemnestra. After Maurie's suspicious death, their children, Owen and Kirsten, assume the roles of Orestes and Electra. Nick Martens, Maurie's best friend and Isabel's lover, as Aegisthus, plays the central character. Ulrich May, Owen's comrade in the "American Silver Doves Revolutionary Army" (375), appears as Pylades in a supporting role. There is a brief and fatal walk-on by Mrs. Salman, the Halleck maid, as the Nurse. Contemporary Washington, D.C., serves as the backdrop for Oates' up-dated drama of murder and revenge, and the lingering spirit of historic John Brown, a remote ancestor of the Hallecks, whom Henry David Thoreau defended as an "angel of light,"[6] figures as the founding father of the American House of Atreus.

Brown, whose moral position in the novel remains even more ambigu-ous than that of the murderer-hero Jules Wendall, is described as "a martyr, a madman, a murderer, a saint, a demon, a brave fearless heroic man, the Wrath of God, the devil's tool" (14). He presides as the chief symbol of the striking ambivalence that structures *Angel of Light*: the thematic examination of violence as both symptom and solution.

The separate narratives of the brother and the sister explore these alternatives. Although their father has died in an automobile accident, Kirsten Halleck manages to convince her brother Owen that Isabel and Nick have colluded in his murder. Together, the teenage siblings try to gather evidence to support their obsessive suspicions, but when it comes to exacting vengeance they act separately. Owen assassinates his mother, and Kirsten attempts to kill Nick Martens.

By joining a revolutionary cell, Owen is able to justify the murder of his mother as a political act. He prepares for Isabel's "execution" by laying out the accouterments of his crime—"his assassin's clothes, the German knife, the loop of fine strong pitiless wire, the dark suede gloves, the taped flashlight, the vial of chloroform, the little red pill box" (379)—like a kid getting ready for camp. After her death he is too overcome by a mysterious lethargy to escape the explosive charge he himself has set, and, cradled in his dead mother's bed, Owen perishes in the detonation.

Leslie Fiedler discovered in the "boy's books," which for him comprise our national literature, "an unintended symbolic confession of the inade-quacy we sense but cannot remedy" (144). Through Owen's boy-narrative, Oates probes inadequate concepts of revolution, but in Kirsten's story she suggests the remedy. In *them* the posturing of self-styled intellectual rebels is contrasted to the popular, manic rage of the Detroit riots, the "fire" that "burns and does its duty" (473). In *Angel of Light* this comparison is further developed. The militant movement to which Owen becomes a convert is flawed not only in its pomposity but in its philosophy. Uli May, the Dove leader who recruits Owen, preaches a dehumanized terrorism of "gesture" (245). Practiced within this theoretical framework, dispassionate violence cannot produce the human "sympathy" (433) Oates deems necessary for radical change; thus Isabel's death is the culmination of a boy's adventure rather than the inauguration of social transfiguration. Oates' presentation of Owen, the soft-bellied intellectual, as a contemporary Orestes dismisses American revolutionary movements as rich kids' games.

But *Angel of Light* also propounds figurative violence as a means of transformation. Like the Electras of Sophocles and Euripides, Kirsten Halleck is characterized by her tenacity and intensity. Unlike that of Owen, Kirsten's is a crime of passion. Instead of a political execution, she plots seduction and retribution. Whereas Owen has attempted to simplify Isabel into an image, what emerges in Kirsten's encounter with Nick is complicated and disturbing humanity. Naked, the suave and handsome Nick is exposed as a "lardy" old man. And Kirsten fails to forsee the "hard work" of murder: "She had not anticipated the simple resistance of flesh. And bone, when struck. Bone! The knife flew from her damp fingers and crashed against the floor" (416). It is Kirsten's crime—fallible and emotional—that physically, graphically, engages the complexity of the human predicament that blunderingly effects the commencement of the reformation of power that the novel demands.

It is the dehumanization of power as an ideological premise that Oates looks to tragedy—human and terrible in its gore—to redress. In her 1972 critical collection on tragic forms in literature, Oates argued for the "affirmation" in violent spectacle: "nihilism is overcome by the breaking-down of the dikes between human beings, the flowing forth of passion" (*The Edge of Impossibility* 11). Rankled, perhaps, by the ubiquitous charge of excessive violence in her fiction, Oates may have wished to further clarify this point in her 1981 work.[7] Nick's recollection of something he and Maurie had read about as boys again propounds the potential of ritualized violence for the creation of human connection:

some brutal religious practices—secret rites—rites of what we would now call initiation—in which young men were terrorized and exhausted to the point of hysteria, so that they lost the self's boundaries, and identified with the very victim of the sacrifice . . . and they would evidently tear at the living flesh with their hands—guzzle blood like hyenas—they passed over into what they were killing— they were the victims—it was a form of sympathy we can't understand. (432–433)[8]

The thematic necessity of the reformation of power by attaching it to some "form of sympathy" makes *Angel of Light* comprehensible in terms of the central project of Oates' fiction, the recasting of an alliance of power and nurturance. The options for this alliance in the upper-class world where authority originates are framed in the contrasting characters of Maurie and Nick. As we observed in the short story "Swamps," Oates frequently divides contradictory definitions of power between father figures, and even in youth Maurie Halleck and Nick Martens represent opposing principles.[9]

Maurie, whose inherited wealth guarantees him a position of authority, abdicates its responsibility. Deeply influenced by the religious vocation of Cardinal de Monnier of Quebec who abandoned his ecclesiastical "power" to go to Africa as a "prayerful witness" (71) to suffering "even when he can't—and often he can't—bring about much change" (73), Maurie represents goodness without force. His life suggests the ideal of morality, but his alcoholic death represents his basic ineffectuality.

Nick, by contrast, the son of a failed artist, seeks power rather than goodness. Nick is the flawed Renaissance man Oates castigates in "The Death Throes of Romanticism" presented as a prep-school boy—athletic, musical, intelligent, popular, class president: "handsome Nick Martens with his wit, his sarcasm, his zest for competition, his plotting, his calculating, his restless mannerisms . . . his tireless self-promotion" (56). Nick is, in brief, what Jules was trying to become. Oates borrows his characteristic features and interests—and the erroneous isolation fundamental to his implied morality—from Ernest Hemingway.[10] Nick is, for example, a champion boxer. And the relationship of Maurie and Nick is set for life on a male-only wilderness canoe trip during which the boys retreat to nature, cook trout, eat with gusto, share nascent philosophies, and swap stories of adolescent experience.

Maurie's submissive stance, despite his saintly sentiments, is an abandonment of responsibility. So he dies. Although Nick abuses his authority, Kirsten's violent attempt on his life apparently reforms him, and so he survives. Recovering from the knife wounds she has inflicted, Nick seems to develop the capacity for the kind of "sympathy" he describes above. The epilogue to the novel finds him alone in his father's seaside cottage. Having confessed to the financial misdealings for which Maurie had allowed himself to be blamed, Nick has refused to explain and thereby justify his actions, and he has turned the mirrors of the cabin to the wall so he does not have to encounter the self—that menacing competitive "I" he has spent his life perfecting. Instead, he has become sensitive to "the emptiness and beauty of a world uncontaminated by, and unguided by, human volition" (428).

Nick spends much of his time writing unmailed letters to Kirsten explaining his transformation: "*I became suddenly generous—but I have very little to give away. And no one who wants it*" (425). Nick's reformation—the movement of the principle of power away from the "volition" of self toward concern for others—links the project of this novel to that of *them*, but Nick's new form, it is emphasized, remains tentative. Although he is struggling to combine the capability of power with the capacity for nurturance, in the symbolic vocabulary of Oates' fiction the motif of the pastoral retreat indicates that the solution Nick represents at the end of *Angel of Light* exists only as a hopeful ideal. *"You've given me life again,"* he writes to Kirsten. *"But what am I to do with it?"* (427).

In rich families or poor, Oates' stories of the induction of brothers and sisters into the operant conditions of power are studies in ideology that expose the evils of the system. In the comic tale, the poor hero must find a way to succeed within a social structure he cannot control. Jules' story points up the pitfalls of this conformist enterprise in a corrupt society. In classic tragedy, on the other hand, the privileged hero, who does have means and resources to shape his world, is supposed to sacrifice himself to reform social corruption. The hostile detachment of Owen and Uli, and Tony Di Piero, their grown-up counterpart, presents the symptoms of a worse abuse of power than the reactive violence defining the adult world Jules encounters, but the silly death of Oates' tragic hero Owen does nothing to rectify it.

Oates' separate treatments of the problem of power in comedy and tragedy indicate class differences. *them* and *Angel of Light* demonstrate that in terms of the levels and types of power classified by Rollo May (40–50), the ineffective personal assertion and desperate aggression by the lower classes is different in kind from the exploitative, manipulative, and competitive exercise of genuine power by the upper classes: although the poor man may resort to angry but necessary self-assertion, the rich man practices dispassionate and widespread destruction.

In Oates' stories of lower-class families, fathers, like Howard Wendall of *them*, frequently respond to their economic reality by lashing out in confused violence, whereas Oates' wealthy fathers operate as agents of the inhumane power deployed by the institutions they serve. In *Do with Me What You Will*, *Wonderland*, and *Angel of Light*, for example, paternal figures represent the detrimental practices of law, medicine, and politics. According to Louis Althusser, modern society is not ordered by direct force; instead its operant conditions are secured through institutions that define and transmit social values (127ff.). To challenge the definitions of power promoted by upper-class professionals, then, is to transform power at its source. The bloody attack on Nick Martens is rooted in this thematic objective.

The business of tragedy is redemption, a utopian project powerfully appealing to Oates' sensibility. The famous sons of prominent families— Hamlet, Oedipus, Orestes, and that ultimate tragic hero, Christ—suffered to save their human communities, but the forms and incidents of that suffering were imposed through the heroes' family relationships. Murder the uncle who beds the mother; kill the father and marry the mother; kill the mother to avenge the father; or die to conform to a father's will: in each of these dramas significant social change was sought through domestic conflict, a pattern at work in Oates' oeuvre as well. In tragedy, Oates argues, it is precisely "the making of domestic landscapes into wilderness . . . that always shocks us" (*The Edge of Impossibility* 8).

But for Oates the redemption possible in classic tragedy cannot be accomplished even by the favored sons of the modern world. In her version, the wealthy brother, like the poor brother of her comedy, is inducted into the violence characteristic of his class. In *Angel of Light* it is the style of that violence—cold and calculating—that disqualifies Owen as sympathetic savior. For this role Oates substitutes the transgressive sister whose impassioned violation of convention introduces tenuous reform at the margin of her text.

"Parody," Oates asserts in her commentary on tragic form, "is an act of aggression. Twentieth-century literature is never far from parody, sensing itself anticipated, overdone, exhausted. But its power lies in the authenticity of its anger" (*The Edge of Impossibility* 11). The parodic siblings of *Angel of Light* honor Oates' double imperative: through the character of her mock-Orestes, Oates aggressively uncovers the exhaustion of the tragic possibility imposed by the corruption of power in contemporary America. And her transgressive mock-Electra manages the anger that must fuel any ambiguous struggle toward redemption at "the edge of impossibility."

REGRESSION REFUSED

Let us imagine for a moment that venerable couple, Clifford Pyncheon and his ancient sister Hepzibah, on their ill-fated flight from the stultifying House of the Seven Gables into the confusing animation of railroad travel: "so like children in their inexperience. . . . They were wandering all abroad, on precisely such a pilgrimage as a child often meditates, to the world's end, with perhaps a sixpence and a bisquit in his pocket" (Hawthorne 199). Or picture Roderick Usher in the cataclysmic death grip of his gruesome sibling.

Rather than the sympathetic passion Oates seeks in tragedy, naiveté and melodrama—attitudes that color Hawthorne's and Poe's presentations of attenuated brother-and-sister relationships—are characteristic of the incest themes of nineteenth-century literature. According to a recent review of the subject, sibling incest "closes out most of the world except the self and what is already in its sway. In a sense it's the most vulgar anarchism. There is little room for development in so narrow and humid a corridor" (Miller 8).

Oates' sibling pairs, however, demonstrate the refusal of this limitation. In the last pages of *them* Maureen explains to Jules that despite her great affection she needs to be entirely separate from him in the future: "you were a wonderful brother to me, and I love you . . . but I want it over with" (477). And despite the bond developed during their mutual project of vengeance, at the conclusion of *Angel of Light* Owen is dead and Kirsten is living in seclusion. Laney and Vale never even encounter one another in the course of *Childwold*, and the relationships of those couples who are as much brothers and sisters as they are lovers are doomed to failure.

This is certainly the case of Shar and Karen of *With Shuddering Fall*. Much of his attraction for her is a shared childhood during which he played the same role of Kess, Jules, and Vale—that of protective big brother. And Shar alludes to an affair between his mother and Karen's father (39), so the young lovers could be actual siblings. Even the lovers of *Do with Me What You Will*, Elena Howe and Jack Morrissey, share a symbolic father. Marvin Howe, Elena's paternalistic husband, is also the man who replaced Jack's actual father in the boy's imagination when Howe was the lawyer in Mr. Morrissey's murder trial. Despite Elena's celebrated awakened passion, I suspect that she and Jack would have to part in order to continue to develop. In fact, whatever the exigencies of plot, the brothers and sisters of Oates' family fiction are, it would seem, fated to separation.

With reference to the structural explanation for Oates' *oeuvre* we are adapting from Jameson's use of Greimas' principles, the brother, excluded from nurturance, and the sister, excluded from power, are "negative or privative terms" (*The Political Unconscious* 168) whose union would not result in resolution of the contradictions the domestic gender system imposes but in "the very caricature of a dialectical resolution . . . merely a horrible object-lesson" (*The Political Unconscious* 169), a lesson the examples from Poe and Hawthorne may provide.

Oates' explanation of the brother-sister plot as it appears in her work may be found in her highly original reading of Emily Brontë's *Wuthering Heights*. "Brontë's emotions," Oates explains, "are clearly caught up with" the "child's predilections" demonstrated by the relationship of Heathcliff and Catherine Earnshaw, but "the greatness of her genius as a novelist allows her a magnanimity, an imaginative elasticity, that challenges the very premises. . . of the Romantic exaltation of the child and childhood's innocence" ("The Magnanimity of *Wuthering Heights*" 68). The deep attachment of Brontë's girl and boy—a sibling love with the intensity of chaste incest—freezes them, Oates argues, into "a single attitude, they *are* an attitude, and can never develop" (78). A second couple, young Catherine and Hareton, supplants the symbolic brother and sister. The relationship of the second couple is marked not by the rigidity and obsession of the first but by maturity and accommodation. So, as the book ends, "suddenly childhood is *past*; it retreats to a darkly romantic and altogether poignant legend, a 'fiction' of surpassing beauty but belonging to a remote time" (80). The great appeal of the first Catherine and her Heathcliff, in Oates' view, is that they give voice to our own preoccupations, "this seductive and deathly centripetal force we all carry within us" (71).

It is tempting to imagine Oates' affectionate brothers and sisters forming alliances that balance oppositions—the stasis of Karen and the movement of Shar, the pessimism of Maureen and the optimism of Jules, the heart of Kirsten and the head of Owen—but Oates' fictions, as we have noted, reject a retreat to romantic and innocent solutions. Oates declines an art of "regressive fantasies": "the role of the superior intellect is not to honor incompletion . . . but to help bring about fulfillment of potentialities" ("The Death Throes of Romanticism" 117). The problems of power Oates' domestic fictions evoke must not be eluded. Brothers and sisters must refuse alliances that stultify growth with familiarity; they must separate to struggle toward completion. The adult limitations that must concern them can be challenged only through their troubled relations with fathers, mothers, and grown-up lovers.

Chapter Four

Fathers and Sons: The Refusal of Violence

The characterological and structural ambiguities of *them* and *Angel of Light* testify to Joyce Carol Oates' continuing ambivalence about violence. But if Oates' comedy and her tragedy equivocally introduce violence as a means of achieving status or sympathy, a significant contradictory pattern may be observed in her father-son narratives: the emergent refusal of violence as solution.

The problem of the son in Oates' works is that he must become an adult male; he will assume the potentialities and the liabilities of the fathers' culturally encoded positions. In Oates' father-and-son novels these problems and potentialities are frequently displayed in the split figure of the father. The most striking feature of the sons' stories in *them*, *A Garden of Earthly Delights*, and *Wonderland* is the presentation of two different kinds of father, whom I shall define as the *actual* and the *ideological*. Just as Oates' treatments of comedy and tragedy explore separate classes, the distinction between the two types of father expresses class difference. Whereas the actual father, with whom the son is most closely identified through birth or early experience, demonstrates the liabilities that result from economic deprivation, the ideological father figures, representatives of the upper classes, seem to offer access to privilege. The actual father has instructed the son in the hazards of impotence, but in the course of each of these novels the son's experience of the ideological father teaches the immorality of power.

Although the device of the two fathers has an impressive history, in Oates' works it points to a contemporary truth. According to Otto Rank in

The Myth of the Birth of the Hero, double paternity is a pattern in the legends of Moses, Romulus, Gilgamesh, and many other cultural heroes. Typically, the protagonist is brought up in obscurity as the son of a poor and humble man only to discover later his true status as the offspring of a royal father. Instead of indicating social elevation, however, Oates' two-father motifs are fictive renditions of the problematic male gender identification that Nancy Chodorow describes in *The Reproduction of Mothering*. Because the primary responsibility for child care falls to mothers in this society, Chodorow argues that a "boy must learn to attempt to develop a masculine gender identification and learn the masculine role in the absence of a continuous and ongoing personal relationship with his father." As a result of this situation, boys both "appropriate those specific components of masculinity that they fear will be used against them" and develop a sense of what it is to be masculine "through identification with cultural images of masculinity and men chosen as masculine models" (176).

Jules, Swan, and Jesse, the sons of *them*, *A Garden of Earthly Delights*, and *Wonderland* introject the defensive rage of their own actual fathers and adopt the means of empowerment modeled by the ideological fathers of these works. The sons' experiences of dual fathers provide a comprehensive examination of the issues of male violence through which Oates moves from characteristic ambivalence toward provisional refusal.

This chapter contends that Oates' treatment of violence must be understood as embedded in the more complex problem of power. Just as Jules of *them* solved the problem of empowerment through recourse to violence, Swan of *A Garden of Earthly Delights* resolves his confusion about the issues of family power through the murder of his ideological father and his own suicide. These strategies define the problem of masculine power without proposing a solution. It is left to Jesse in the revised ending of *Wonderland* to struggle toward a revision of the modes of his serial fathers without resorting to their characteristic violence.

TWO FATHERS

The folk device of the two fathers is introduced in *them* in terms of actual possibility through Jules' conception, the first significant event in the novel. When teenage Loretta allows Bernie Malin to share her bed, he is murdered before dawn by her brother Brock, and that morning policeman Howard Wendall comes to her rescue, for a price—sexual intercourse. Thus two possible fathers for the child who is born nine months later make Jules' paternity questionable. Although Loretta marries Howard and the baby is raised as his son, she hints frequently at the deep mystery of Jules' identity (59, 106), and the possibility of alternative fathers provides Jules with antithetical definitions of power. Like the young son in "Swamps" whose father represents submission to economic authority, Jules experiences in Howard Wendall, his actual father, frustration of self-significance as a response to economic necessity, which in Howard's case is expressed as petty viciousness within the family circle.

Jules' other father exists, since he died in youth, only as veiled hint—the pull of legend. His mysterious presence encourages identification with the heroes of romance. Jules, then, like most boys raised in this society seeks his masculine identity through the popular images of the ideological father. As Chodorow argues, young males "tend to identify with a cultural stereotype of the masculine role" (176). So invested is Jules in this identification with the images of popular culture that he thinks of himself as a character in a book, "a fictional fifteen-year-old with the capacity to become anything, because he was a fiction" (99). "This looks like Chapter One," Jules confidently announces to Bernard Geffen (235). The problem is, however, that it is really the book that writes the character: "what was his personal history might have been stolen from movies and books" (358–359). Lingering by the movie theater after Howard Wendall's death, Jules gazes at the posters of his ideological heroes and wonders "if these faces would someday betray him" (133). As the analysis of the failure of Jules' cultural models in the last chapter reveals, his story is largely the account of that betrayal.

Like Jules' story, *A Garden of Earthly Delights* is a novel suspended between two figures of the father. Carleton Walpole, with whom the story begins, is an extreme example of the lower-class father. An itinerant fruit picker, he has no property and, as a result, no control over the conditions of his work. This lack of control is symbolized by the shifting locations of his labor, and, as we noted in Chapter 1, his perpetual dislocation of place is symbolic of a profound dislocation of spirit. Carleton represents the paternal style of submission to economic authority. When he resorts to violence it is as a response to forces that he does not understand. When he kills his best friend Rafe in a barroom brawl, for example, he is as much victim as agent of the contingent violence that defines him.

The figure of Curt Revere, Carleton's opposite, dominates the last section of the novel. Like Karen's father in *With Shuddering Fall*, Revere is the head of a rural empire; he owns gypsum mines, farm land, a factory, and a lumber yard. But more important, as his adopted son Swan understands, is the power such ownership confers. For Revere, violence is both a metaphor and a means of his characteristic control. He is the kind of man to whom a gun is a "natural . . . extension of his hand or fist" (295).

Other important characters in the novel—Lowry, Clara, and Swan—
exist in relation to these extreme positions. Lowry, who is another one of
Oates' symbolic older brothers, rescues Clara when she runs away from
her father, Carleton, to protect her own limited autonomy, but although he
eventually becomes Clara's lover and the biological father of her child,
the bond between them remains tenuous. For, like Carleton, Lowry is a
traveler. As he confesses to Clara, like her, he grew up in a sort of migrant
farm family. But unlike Carleton, Lowry tries to control his own life. A
rum runner in the early part of the story, he drives, rather than be driven
like Carleton, and he also attempts to take charge of his life through
comprehending it. Unlike Carleton who dies without having been able to
"think" (115) the fragments of his experience into some order, Lowry seeks
control through education. He counsels Clara to learn to read to achieve
the power her own family lacked. But because Clara is Lowry's sister in
her similar deficiency of knowledge, he cannnot make her his wife.
Instead, he marries a "teacher" who he had hoped would help him clarify
his thoughts.

But no amount of knowledge could help Lowry organize the explosion
of experience he encounters in Europe during the Second World War. Like
Vale of *Childwold*, he is apparently both physically and emotionally
damaged when he returns to reclaim Clara in Swan's fourth year. In spite
of her passionate love for Lowry, Clara senses his insufficiency and rejects
him because of the "weakness" they share (243). Towheaded Lowry,
whom blond Clara so resembles in physical appearance, is the brother to
her lack of power, so a union between them would solve the problems of
neither.

The section of the novel that bears Lowry's name is situated symbolically between the stories of Carleton and Revere. And Clara, whose story
runs throughout the novel, also occupies the symbolic space between the
impotence of Carleton and the power of Revere, although at sixteen, she
believes that she "took her life into control" (189). Abandoned by the
unreliable Lowry and pregnant with his child, Clara begins a relationship
with the stable Revere, a forty-year-old rich man who is attracted to her.
He thinks her son, whom she nicknames Swan, is his own child, and he
provides for both of them until the death of his first wife in Swan's sixth
year. It is not until then that Clara's marriage establishes both mother and
son as official members of the Revere family.

Clara's ambiguous social position as Revere's longtime mistress stands,
however, for her vulnerable situation halfway between Carleton's submission and Revere's control. Because as a woman in Oates' novel she is
limited to the feminine devices of passion and acquiescence and can never

claim Revere's stability, wealth, and position as her own, Clara projects this ambition onto her young son. Unlike Carleton, who must harvest only for others, Clara, one of Oates' fallen goddesses, tends a garden of domestic plants for her own pleasure, but that garden remains the property of Curt Revere. It is Clara's suspension between insecurity and stability that fuels her urgent plans for her son. On the day of her wedding when Swan exhibits his fear of his "new father" (264) and his apprehension about his three new brothers, Clara predicts, "You're going to take everything away from them someday and kick them out of this house. . . . Someday you'll get back at him—you'll be his best son" (263).

Swan, who loves his mother, unquestioningly accepts her charge, a pact comparable to that between father and daughter in *With Shuddering Fall*, and equally disastrous. Intelligent and intuitive, his first step is to assess the power relationships within his new family. Revere has a clear and devastating effect on his mother; in Swan's eyes he is, therefore, omnipotent. Swan is terrified at the way Clara changes in Revere's presence: "no one anywhere . . . had such power over Clara as that man" (266).

By the time he is a young man Swan acknowledges his own desperation for power: he aches for power as if it were food (345), and all he has to do to get it is be his father's son. But that is precisely the problem. Like the other key characters in the novel, Clara's son is also suspended between two fathers. His two different names signify that suspension: his public identity of Steven Revere is contradicted by his "real name," Swan Walpole (326). In contrast to Jules in *them*, Swan lives with Revere, his ideological father, whom he expects to emulate, but it is his actual father, Lowry, whom he encounters only once, who haunts his destiny as surely as Jules' fictive heroes impel him.

What distinguishes Lowry from Revere is the issue of violence. Violence is for Revere a natural right, a positive mark of his masculinity, an attitude that finds expression in his insistence that Swan learn to hunt. But for the contemplative Lowry, who has experienced its extreme escalation as war, violence represents both male fate and male shame. His only words to his son address this central issue. "You ever killed any snakes or things, kid?" he interrogates little Swan, who fearfully shakes his head "No." "You're lying. I can see in your face you killed something already and you're going to kill lots of things. . . . I can see it right there—all the things you are going to kill and step on and walk over" (247).

Like Jules, who tried and failed to escape sharing Howard's deadly anger, Swan tries, yet fails, to avoid the consequences of his actual father's prediction, but his attempt to assume his position as the son of his ideological father first involves the boy in a hunting accident that kills his brother, and finally results in Swan's murder of Revere and his own suicide.

When Swan is ten years old he is subjected to pressure that originates with Revere: he will hunt and he will like it. Clara placates her husband with the promise that Swan will learn to shoot, despite her knowledge of his antipathy for hunting and his gentle affection for animals. But Swan does go hunting with his thirteen-year-old brother Robert because he understands that killing is the price he has to pay for Revere's acceptance. Murdering small creatures, Swan knows, is "playing at being men" (301). This masculine game turns more serious, however, when Swan strikes his brother in anger as they are crossing a pasture. Robert's gun gets entangled in a barbed wire fence, discharging to wound him fatally, and in spite of the family pressure and the accidental circumstances, Swan is never able to fully disclaim moral culpability for his brother's death.

Swan's motivation is even more obscure in the murder of Revere. In *The Tragic Vision of Joyce Carol Oates*, Sister Mary Kathryn Grant contends that violence in Oates' work is the end result of impotence that is often expressed as love. For her, Swan's violent act is the furious outcome of a lifetime of maternal manipulation. Intending to kill Clara, he is unable to stammer out a reason, so she herself supplies the degrading explanation: "You're weak, that's what I know about you."(382). Swan's final actions, according to Grant, seem to support Clara's accusation. Unable to murder his mother, Swan suddenly "turns the gun on Revere, killing him, and then himself: his powerlessness complete" (48).

According to this unsatisfactory interpretation, Revere's importance in the symbolic structure of the story is negligible—he is killed merely by default. Yet his death has paramount significance in an ideological consideration of the text. For Curt Revere, as Clara realizes, is not finally "a private, intimate human being" (290); even within the personal relationships of his own family, he is not so much a man as a figure who stands for a competitive, acquisitive style, which Swan, his last remaining son, is not only "equal to" (361) but on the verge of surpassing at the conclusion of the novel.

Revere's connection with all his sons is so cold and domineering that the whole family looks to Clara to intervene with him on all domestic issues, but, for young Swan, Revere's distant paternal style exceeds the merely personal. When Revere reads his family the stark tales of the Old Testament, Swan sees "in his father's blunt graying head a shadow of God Himself" (313).

As a child, Swan conceives of Revere as a terrible God who presided over a brutal and greedy universe: "Lurking over everything was the spirit of God, restless and haunting; it would swoop down now and then like a bird of prey, like a chicken hawk, and seize someone in its beak" (313). On the fatal day of his last hunt, Robert shoots a chicken hawk, but Swan's brief "rush of hope" for the weaker birds that seem to flock to witness its defeat is replaced by the hopeless realization that they too are part of the omnipresent cycle of plunder and violence.

Swan's murder of his ideological father is no accident; it should be read as the symbolic rejection of the violent and exploitative power Revere represents. And Swan's suicide is the hopeless realization of himself as the weaker bird that is, nonetheless, an active and reprehensible participant in a chicken-hawk world.

After the murder-suicide at the climax of the novel, Clara lives out the remainder of her long life in a dazed condition. The last words of *A Garden of Earthly Delights* describe her as being most content when she is watching television

programs that showed men fighting . . . shooting guns and driving fast cars, killing the enemy again and again until the dying gasps of evil men were only a certain familiar rhythm away from the opening blasts of the commercials. (384)

Clara's great comfort in the familiarity of these themes indicates that the world of competitive commercial violence is the meaning at the core of the life of the Revere family; the ultimate meaning of "all" that Swan "had inherited" (363), then, is what Lowry had predicted for him—a heritage of things to be killed and walked over. Swan's murder of his father and his destruction of the son deliberately created in that father's image must be understood as more than the insane resolution of his personal mistreatment by an ambitious mother: it is the violent refusal of a crude capitalistic male ideology of unmitigated power.

SERIAL FATHERS

Wonderland is a work of extraordinary energy. In *A Garden of Earthly Delights*, Swan refuses one figure who represents the definition of power inherent in capitalism, but in *Wonderland* Jesse Harte-Pedersen-Vogel refuses an encyclopedic series of related ideologies represented by the father figures of the novel. According to Ellen Friedman's reading, Oates

has taken her protagonist through major events in a thirty-two-year period of American history in which he encounters figures who offer violence, solipsism, megalomania, empiricism, behaviorism, Manicheanism, sensualism, and nihilism as paths of truth in order to point to the redeeming path of love, which requires a recognition that the world is larger than the single ego. (15)

Friedman also believes, however, that Jesse's protean encounters render him "kingly" (110). Although agreeing in tactic with Friedman's interpretation of serial encounters, I intend to demonstrate that Jesse's significance lies less in reaching some pinnacle of power than in its reformulation. Thus, my analysis will differ in emphasizing his relationships with male figures as representing various strategies of paternal control. It is, I believe, Oates' achievement in this important novel to imaginatively transform the concept of power from exploitative to nutrient through the episodic refusals that define her protagonist.

Jesse's actual father, Willard Harte, like Carleton Walpole and Howard Wendall, is a victim of economic forces beyond his control or comprehension. During the Christmas season of his fourteenth year, Jesse senses a terrible tension in his family that exists in contrast to the anticipated celebration. His mother is glowing with the new life of her fifth pregnancy, but his father is heard stomping angrily about in the dark. On the thirteenth of December, 1939, Willard has finally had to nail a crude "Closed" sign on his failed gas station. On December 14, he unexpectedly picks up Jesse early from his after-school job, and, when father and son enter the house, Jesse literally steps into the spilled blood of his murdered family. Frightened and confused, he escapes out a back window, but while he is running across the open field, Jesse is injured by a blast from his father's shotgun, which Willard later turns upon himself.

The Harte tragedy provides a graphic illustration of Grant's thesis of violence as the culmination of impotence. Unable to achieve economic autonomy, Willard Harte violently subdues the only thing he can control: his own family. Stark power in conflict with necessary nurturance, the general predicament in all Oates' families, is, as a result, concretely realized as the paradoxical problem of Jesse's existence. As the only survivor of Harte's murderous frustration, throughout his life Jesse seeks modes of power, means of control, that can protect him from the father's impotent but deadly rage without overwhelming the mother's love and connection he is also seeking. However, because, as Oates' works demonstrate, contemporary family arrangements do not promote this ideal balance, the male systems of control Jesse learns from his various adoptive fathers are consistently undermined by his sympathy for the females to whom he is drawn during the course of the novel.

Grandfather Vogel is Jesse's first ideological father. While Jesse is recovering from his gunshot wound, the backbreaking hard work and perpetual silence of his grandfather's farm accommodate the numbness and withdrawal of his emotional condition as a "survivor" (64).[1] *"Closer to those dead animals"* he finds after the spring thaw *"than to the living dog"* (57), Jesse is at first so deeply traumatized that he is even disturbed by the noisy liveliness of Duke, the family pet who also survived the attack by Harte. But as Jesse gradually comes back to life himself, he becomes aware of the life-denying negation of the self-imposed isolation within his grandfather's stance of pioneer independence. When Jesse longs to have access to the Harte family possessions Vogel has locked up in a storage barn, the grandfather breaks the protective silence between them with ugly accusations that connect the suffering son to his dead mother: "'You're like *her*,' the old man said suddenly, sneering. . . . 'You don't let trouble alone, you hunt it out'" (61). In reaction against his grandfather's angry misanthropy, Jesse seeks a sense of affectionate connection with his lost family. He flees the farm, running back to the Harte home to spend the night in the empty shadows imagining, longing for the return of his squabbling siblings and his earthy mother.

With his next ideological father Jesse emerges from the speechless, defensive character he assumed at his grandfather's farm and maintained at the home of his aunt and uncle and at the orphanage to which he was subsequently sent to learn another form of empowerment—power through incorporation—the style amply represented by Dr. Karl Pedersen. Pedersen, a physician whom his wife accuses of taking over his patients' minds and souls, certainly intends to assimilate Jesse, his "adopted" son, whose survival demonstrates resilience, an adaptive quality Pedersen has too succesfully eradicated in his own overcontrolled family of "freaks" (120).

Pedersen's philosophy grafts a doctrine of familial manifest destiny onto a belief in social progress. Control and extraordinary effort are the keys to "fate," which has to be molded through diligent planning, intensive education, and steadfast faith in acquisitive advancement. In *Bellefleur*, Oates reports, she hoped to present "a microcosm of America—imperialistic, exploitative, yet tirelessly optimistic" ("Speaking about Short Fiction" 98). The Pedersen family of *Wonderland* is her first exercise in this intention.

Man's "destiny" is to "claim new territory" (113), Pedersen preaches. Lockport will "expand" and property values "will rise" (115), Pedersen predicts. He himself is "straining to be God," to occupy "God's place, to take from Him all that He will allow me to take. I am a perfect protoplasm" (109), he proclaims. The book's metaphor for all this expansion is the enormous consumption of food that literally transforms the Pedersens into giants. In order to be Pedersen's son, to someday fill his "place" (98), young Jesse has a lot of catching up to do. All day long he is required to stuff his mind with educational facts as voraciously as he fills his body with immense quantities of food at the Pedersen table, where he is expected to provide a daily and detailed report of his intellectual "progress" (83).

Jesse's reason for all this gorging is, however, fundamentally different from that of his new father. Pedersen is hungry for power, whereas Jesse is starved for love. When he is in Mrs. Pedersen's kitchen, his feeling of warm acceptance makes his new identity of Jesse Pedersen seem real to him. This feeling of belonging is somehow connected with the food she gives him, and as he wanders the streets of Lockport feeling empty of a sense of connection, a great hunger for all the nourishment she provides grows within him.

It is not surprising, then, that when he discovers the split between power and love in the Pedersen family—Mrs. Pedersen is the loving victim of her husband's power—Jesse attempts to come to her aid in a grotesque attempt at rescue. Fortified with two Chinese take-out dinners, several candy bars, "six hamburgers with chili sauce, three side dishes of french fries" (182), and two bottles of Coke, Jesse learns that in retaliation for his efforts on his mother's behalf, a second father has tried to obliterate him. Pedersen has rescinded his fatherhood: "With this check and this letter I pronounce you dead to me. You have no existence. You are nothing" (183).

If Pedersen personifies the jingoistic expansionism of American attitudes during World War II, Jesses's next ideological fathers, as Friedman suggests, represent scientific attitudes dominating the 1950s and the 1960s (105). After the loss of his second family, Jesse assumes his grandfather's name, Vogel, which signals the defensive psychological attitude of his adult life—remoteness. But this time it is the remoteness endorsed by science. Like Karl Pedersen, Jesse does become a physician, but unlike his second ideological father, Jesse's principal objective is not the incorporation of his environment but the emotional safety afforded by mechanistic control: "He felt his body becoming mechanical, predictable, very sane" (191). The difference between them is marked in Jesse's personal habits: during his years as a medical student, eating, the dominant symbolic mode of the Pedersen family, is repulsive to him, and eating in the "presence of others" impossible (189). Jesse's beliefs are influenced at this stage by the paternal figure of Benjamin Cady, the Nobel Prize-winning neurochemist who becomes first his mentor, then his father-in-law. According to Cady, people fear "mechanisms" because they do not know that they are "mechanisms themselves" (191). Contemplating Cady's remarks, Jesse concludes that the object of science is something he feels very much in need of: "*Control. That was all he wanted*" (195).

The darker side of Cady's philosophy is not directly presented in the novel but figuratively developed through the apalling projection "Trick" Monk. Despite Jesse's attraction to the regulation of science, he still recognizes and acts upon his need for human connection. "I imagine myself this way," he explains. "There will be my own family, my wife and children . . . the work I do, the patients I see . . . will be a kind of family to me also" (209). Jesse's relation to his landlady during his student days is familial, and his desire to marry Anne-Marie and his marriage to Helene Cady testify that despite his remoteness he values love. But his need to dominate Anne-Marie and his sense of her as sexually dirty reveal the scientific Jesse who wishes only to order and purify. His marriage to Cady's daughter, a woman in whom intellectual talent seems to preclude passion, is a compromise that honors the competing needs of his character.

Trick—another medical student, who resembles Jesse in age and appearance—functions as a kind of negative double who expresses the implications of the side of Jesse that seeks domination through science. Monk, a "trickster," whose clownish pose grants him "license to say anything," expresses, for example, envy at the opportunity for experimentation enjoyed by Nazi doctors: "Imagine. . . . cats with handles. . . . You must admit that Hitler had a certain style, a certain flair" (206). The "fooling around" (239), the antic horror of the animal experimentation farm to which Trick escorts Jesse and Helene, and his revelation of tasting a human uterus are startling symbols of the displacement of human values by science. But although Jesse champions his humanity when he fights Trick off after a particularly outrageous confrontation, Trick's strong attachment implies that his perverse morality may stand for the unacknowledged "joker" in Jesse's own character.

The depersonalization exhibited by Trick is articulated by Dr. Perrault, the neurosurgeon who is Jesse's last ideological father. When Jesse, his pregnant wife, and his famous father-in-law are invited to dinner at Perrault's home, Jesse feels the familiar double pull of the attraction to the connection of family relationship—he finds himself jealous of Perrault's real children—and to a philosophical position that allows the scientist even more control than Cady's empiricism. Perrault is a behaviorist who argues that the human brain is exclusively composed of "brute matter" and "electrical impulses": "With a tiny pin in my fingers . . . I can destroy any personality in thirty seconds, sixty seconds at the most" (336), he declares.

Perrault's position is far more inhumane than that of Cady, who believes in an observable residue of human personality. Helene is so disturbed by his pronouncements that she calls her host a murderer and becomes physically ill, but Jesse himself feels a "strange thrill of certainty" (336) at his words and eventually joins the older doctor in his lucrative medical practice. But even Jesse, whom Perrault refers to as "My six-foot self" (309), is troubled by a philosophy that allows Perrault to describe a brain operation as a success despite the fact that the seventeen-year-old patient has evidently lost his mind (323).

After his confrontation with Trick Monk, Jesse affirms his commitment to human values through his marriage to Helene. The implications of his relationship to Perrault are resolved more enigmatically in his compelling attraction to Reva Denk. It is five-thirty in the morning toward the end of his grueling twenty-four hour shift as intern in a large metropolitan hospital when Jesse is awakened to attend a case that has stunned everyone in the emergency room. A man in his early thirties, brought in bleeding from a deep wound in his groin, has evidently attempted to castrate himself with a knife. He is accompanied by a lovely and blood-splashed young woman whom Jesse later encounters on the street. Although he never remembers where he met Reva, he feels like her intimate. After their second encounter, he falls immediately and obsessively in love with her despite the fact that on the morning of their first meeting he has become a father and, as he subsequently confides to her, he is "permanently married" (326).

Nevertheless, when the elusive Reva seeks him out at Perrault's office to arrange an abortion, Jesse decides to rescue her. He follows her to Wisconsin and they agree that he will get a divorce, become the father of her unborn child, and "never see" his wife and daughters again (374). In preparation for the consummation of his passion for Reva, Jesse rents a small cabin where he is intending to bathe. There he finds an old razor blade and accidentally nicks himself while he is attempting to shave with it. "[F]ascinated" by his own streaming blood, Jesse deliberately cuts himself again and again, first his chest, then his stomach, and finally, "reverently, he drew the blade through the tangle of pubic hair" (378). Still bleeding, Jesse puts on his clothes and drives home to his family.

To understand Reva's attraction and Jesse's peculiar behavior we will consider Fredric Jameson's theory of art as the imaginary resolution of real contradictions. Jameson's theory rests on formulations of Claude Levy-Strauss for which the interpretation of the distinctive facial decorations of the Caduveo Indians is the key example. If one imagines the faces of these Indians as divided in half, on one side of that division a symmetrical design is displayed, with an assymetrical design on the other. Levi-Strauss contends that the visually opposing motifs are an expression of the contradictory systems that organize Caduveo society. "Since they were unable to come to consciousness" of this contradiction "and to live it," Jameson quotes Levi-Strauss, "they began to dream it" (*Marxism and Form* 384).[2]

The contradiction with which Jesse struggles in *Wonderland* is the opposition between male power and female connection, the Oatesian predicament of family. Reva, as her name suggests, is a dream of resolution that gives expression to both aspects of the dilemma. A related metaphor of both opposing terms is the manifold motif of blood, which represents the chaos of death as well as the rhythmic assertion of continuing life— both the baffling evidence of the deaths of Jesse's family ("blood, drifts of hair like field grass, stiff with blood" [42]) and the emblem of his own survival ("the certainty of . . . his return to himself . . . the inescapable beat of his heart" [62]). For Jesse, blood is a disturbing personal symbol of family: both the maternal principle of connection—the heritage of shared "blood"—and the paternal expression of power as bloody exploitation.

Through the practice of medicine Jesse is able to counter the symbol of blood as acute disorder with its meaning as a force of life: "how he wanted to help them. . . . He could crawl into bed with them, matching his length against theirs. Hook himself up to them. . . . His strong heartbeat would encourage theirs" (297). But medicine also allows Jesse to elude the meaning of his own destructive experience. On the occasion of his first encounter with Reva, he is able, for example, to repair her mutilated companion and evade the frightening implications of his brutal act. Looking around the bloody room after the successful operation, Jesse observes that "everything seemed to him manageable now, in his power, a sacred area he had mastered. *Nobody is going to die*" (302).

Yet, clearly, despite his evasion, again and again Jesse does recognize the deathliness of male power. His repeated attempts to rescue the women in his life bear witness to his unconscious awareness of a situation that his conscious attitudes repeatedly disavow. And in the physical evidence of castration, Jesse is faced with what his actual father's action was an attempt to contradict: the deadly impotence motivating the violent assertion of power. Jesse's medical performance on this occasion, then, is more than the denial of death; it is a denial of the death that he has discovered at the core of the practice of fatherhood.

Reva's fatal attraction is that she brings to the surface Jesse's deeply repressed formulation of family. The circumstances of Jesse's acquaint-ance with her recall the shadow marriage he has managed to forget—the beautiful mother stained with blood by the awful violence of the castrated and castrating father. Jesse's own act of self-mutilation is not a solution to the unbearable contradiction he lives but a nightmare resolution as Jameson defines it, a symbolic display of the pain of his own dilemma. Jesse's blood is a gesture of communion through which he is returned to the family that is united in the bloody death that has excluded him, but the gushing forth of the blood is also an acceptance of his own capacity for survival.

Jesse's blood bath is a complex sign that he must recognize, not elude through subjugating systems of control, his own participation in the complex human situation. But the gesture of castration, which parallels Reva's and Helene's wishes for abortion, is a symbolic refusal of the gender roles that make the human family an unbearable situation. More than the admission of the terrifying impotence concealed by power, Jesse's tentative castration is a refusal of the definitions of power offered by his serial fathers. Since Jesse binds his wounds and returns to his family, his action does not imply a refusal of fatherhood, but, as the last section of the novel indicates, Jesse does come to refuse the practices through which Oates suggests fatherhood is defined and deformed.

In an effort to impress Karl Pedersen, young Jesse learned the definition of homeostasis, the medical concept that describes the living being as able to modify itself slightly in response to external stimuli in order to maintain its essential stability. Although critics claim that Oates' novel endorses this model of constant readjustment to maintain control and consistency (Waller 152, Friedman 103), Jesse's story actually demonstrates, instead, the value of erratic and repeated dislocation to achieve transformation. Ernest Jones explains that Freud's early formulation of the conservative pleasure principle, which Jones compares to medical homeostasis, had to be replaced by the theory of "repetition compulsion" to account for the recurrent anxiety dreams of war neurotics (268–269). A similar pattern of necessary replacement is at work in this novel. Seeking only to adjust to the conditions set by his various adoptive fathers, Jesse, in spite of his conscious intentions, repeatedly enacts the contradictions that make such conformity impossible. The structure of Wonderland is the cycle of nightmare. Harte, Vogel, Pedersen, Cady, Perrault, and, in the last section of the novel, Noel are recurrent components of the same bad dream of the father as persecutor. Mrs. Harte, Mrs. Pedersen, Reva, and, finally Jesse's daughter Shelley are recurrent components of Jesse's revery of the liberation of the victims of the father's rage.

Comparing it to Freud's theory, Oates defines Yeats' concept of "dreaming-back," in an essay appearing a year before the publication of Wonderland, as the ritualized re-experience of "certain events in one's past life again and again in order to be purged of them" (reprinted in The Edge of Impossibility 157). In the novel, Jesse's daughter employs this technique to try to rid herself of her father's influence. In order to dominate Shelley himself, her boyfriend Noel, the Manson-like head of a hippie family, insists she free herself from Jesse: "He told me I could forget you by dreaming back over you and writing it down" (402). *Wonderland* consists in large part of Jesse's nightmare recollections of his fathers. His own dreaming-back is the attempt to liberate himself from their modes of power, which he achieves symbolically through his rescue of Shelley from Noel in the last book of the novel.

Book Three begins and ends with the theme of the dissolution of fatherhood. In the first chapter Shelley, a teenage runaway, writes a letter describing her urgent intention to struggle free of Jesse despite the longing voice within her that whispers, *"Father I want to come home"* (381). Her letters also introduce Noel as an unavoidable embodiment of the anti-father whom Jesse has always tried to evade or deny. Not unlike Jesse's fathers, Noel almost succeeds in destroying Shelley in the name of love. The second chapter presents the theme of the cultural dissolution of fatherhood through the emblematic event of John Kennedy's death, which instills in Jesse a sense of "panic" and the conviction that in "mourning the President" he was "mourning something else—but he did not know what" (399). And Book Three concludes with the culmination of these personal and social themes of the dissolution of fatherhood in Jesse's refusal of the prerogatives of his various fathers and the resultant tentative transformation of the role.

After a series of letters that reveal only the details of Shelley's dangerous physical and mental disintegration—she is deathly ill with drug-induced hepatitis—one letter arrives containing the name of a city, a street, and a restaurant through which Jesse is able to locate her. Jesse sets out to find Shelley, rejecting the isolation he learned from his first ideological father, Grandfather Vogel. The cancerlike chaotic life of Toronto's Yonge Street during the 1960s deeply offends Jesse's instinct for rigid order, yet instead of clinging to the scientific control learned from Cady and Perrault, subsequent ideological fathers, Jesse acts upon the advantages of spontaneity. He buys casual clothing, and leaving behind the costume of Dr. Vogel, he also discards his wallet containing the documentation of his identity. The new Jesse is neither the incorporative father like Karl Pedersen, whom Shelley, like Swan, fears in the image of a devouring bird, nor a murderous father like Willard Harte.

In the version of the ending that first appeared, Jesse purchased the desperately ill Shelley from Noel for five hundred dollars, the price a medical school will pay for a cadaver. Not only was Shelley unlikely to live, but this conclusion implied that Jesse had retained the deadly control deriving from a paternal position rooted in financial power. But in the second version of the ending, which Oates reports she felt compelled to write,[3] refusing to act on his desire to kill Noel with the pistol and knife he carries, Jesse rescues Shelley without incorporative purchase and without murderous violence: "Nobody is going to die tonight" (478), Jesse declares, echoing his statement in the operating room after he met Reva. But this time he is reaching into his resources of human connection rather than asserting authoritarian control.

In the last words of the novel, Shelley reiterates Noel's accusation that Jesse is "the devil," that is, the father who is the incarnation of domination and rage. "Am I?" Jesse asks (479), but in "dreaming-back" over the institution of fatherhood and acting to refuse its serial abuses, Jesse is attempting to reject this designation. By refusing the violence at the heart (Harte) of fatherhood, Jesse substitutes Rollo May's concept of nutrient power for the exploitative power[4] he learned from his ideological fathers.

THE USES OF VIOLENCE

In 1972 Joyce Carol Oates described *Wonderland* as "probably an immoral novel" that she would "never reread" ("Transformations of Self" 58). Not long after its publication she confided to Joe David Bellamy that writing *Wonderland* had left her in "a state of spiritual exhaustion": "It's the first novel I have written that doesn't end in violence, that doesn't liberate the hero through violence, and therefore there is a sickish, despairing, confusing atmosphere about it ("The Dark Lady of American Letters" 23).

Oates' extraordinary repudiation of what is obviously one of her finest and most ambitious works demands analysis. At the center of Oates' fiction is the problem of power, but that problem has two components: the morality of power relations and the necessity of empowerment. Oates' remarks about *Wonderland* suggest the strain between the two objectives.

Oates' father-son novels treat the morality of power relations. Violent, distant, ruthless, incorporative, and controlling—the fathers represent deployments of power that these narratives first try to destroy and finally attempt to reform by imagining power joined to nurturance, as occurs tentatively at the conclusion of *Angel of Light*. The books that portray the uncomfortable relationships of father and son chart this thematic progression. *A Garden of Earthly Delights* resolves the capitalistic violence of the father through another act of violence, but Jesse seeks to solve the problem of fatherhood through the refusal of violence that Oates so uneasily achieves in the ending of *Wonderland*.

Oates' emotional investment in her defense of Jules' "success" in her 1973 comments about *them* is indicative of the centrality of the second issue of power, the necessity of empowerment. Her continuing interest in this issue is most evident in her 1988 extended essay *On Boxing*. For Oates this sport is "America's tragic theater" (116), and the play is the edifying enactment of the underdog hero's battle for achievement and significance. Whatever the gender of the protagonists, however, the issue of empowerment is the problem of the daughters, and the urgency of that problem in Oates' fiction insures the retention of violence as the dual symbol of intense frustration and projected possibilities that persists in the important modalities of transgression to be presented in the next two chapters.

Chapter Five

Transgression I: Mother-Son Romance

Tony Tanner argues in *Adultery in the Novel: Contract and Transgression* that the "real, if secret interest [of the novel] has been aroused by the weak points of the family, the possible fissures, the breaches, the breakdowns" (371). My last three chapters demonstrate that it is the ideologically expected relationships between family members—mother and daughter, sister and brother, father and son—that are the sites for those "breaches" in Oates' novels that I have designated *refusals*—the refusal of innocence, the refusal of substitute relationship, and the refusal of violence. In this chapter and the next I turn to the description of another style of subversion, occurring in Oates' domestic fiction at the opposite juncture, the unexpected relationships of mothers and sons and fathers and daughters: the operation of transgression. Sons and daughters are expected to assume the gender characteristics of the same-sex parents, which provokes evasion of conformity through refusal. The relation to opposite-sex parents demonstrates, on the other hand, the exclusion from gender privilege. The maturing son is excluded from nurturance; the daughter is excluded from power, situations that provoke the elaborate challenge I define as *transgression*.

"Very often," according to Tanner, "the novel writes of contracts but dreams of transgressions" (386). Oates' works participate in the gradual tendency in the developing novel form to foreground this dream of transgression. An obvious step in this evolution is the *anti-hero* of modern fiction: the protagonist who, in the words of the *Harper Handbook to Literature*, is "not simply a failed hero but a social misfit, graceless, weak, often comic, the embodiment of ineptitude and bad luck in a world apparently made for others" (Frye, Baker, and Perkins 39). As Ihab Hassan explains, the "Hero, who once figured as Initiate, ends up as Rebel or Victim" (9). In the modern novel, the presentation of this anti-hero generally places him in counterrelation to the social structure that produces him. Although Oates' transgressive works make use of the convention of the maladroit, defiant, abused hero of modern fiction, they also recognize the impossibility of the superimposition of an imaginary counterstructure. Whereas the anti-hero, like Ralph Ellison's "invisible man," stages his protest by defining a metaphoric space of freedom and moving outside the system, the transgressive protagonist, unable to dream of lighting out for any territory, however surreal, repeatedly inscribes his or her discomfort from within.

For Michel Foucault, transgression implies a connection more complex than the antithesis of two terms; its purpose, like the repeated violations in Oates' works, is to reveal, instead, the dysfunctional interaction between the terms: "Transgression, then, is not related to the limit as black to white, the prohibited to the lawful, the outside to the inside. . . . Rather their relationship takes the form of a spiral which no simple infraction can exhaust" ("Preface to Transgression" 35). By exhibiting such relationships Oates' narratives of transgression articulate the terms and interrogate the limits they impose. The victimization and ineffective rebelliousness of Oates' transgressive protagonists serve to expose the system that creates them.

As a representative instance of Oates' employment of transgression we will consider the 1973 short story "Stalking." Gretchen, the protagonist, is female, a fact that forces us from the outset to recast the convention of the anti-hero as a problem of gender. Our first glimpse of her indicates her problematic situation:

She is dressed for the hunt, her solid legs crammed into old blue jeans, her big, square, strong feet jammed into white leather boots that cost her mother forty dollars not long ago, but are now scuffed and filthy with mud. Hopeless to get them clean again, Gretchen doesn't give a damn. (*Marriages and Infidelities* 147)

Gretchen is uncomfortably suspended between contradictory ascriptions of gender. Unlike the male anti-hero whose failure is marked by weakness, the transgressive heroine here suffers from inappropriate strength. Like the ugly step-sister at the royal ball she cannot contract her foot to any comfortable relation to the female apparel whose value is defined by the social system and promoted by her mother, and hence she cannot claim her feminine reward. Her size, her shape, and her manner violate clear demarcation between conventional masculine and feminine identification, an interpretation reinforced by this detailed description of Gretchen's face:

She has untidy, curly hair that looks like a wig set loosely on her head. Light brown curls spill out everywhere, bouncy, a little frizzy, a cascade, a tumbling of curls. Her eyes are deep set, her eye-brows heavy and dark. She has a stern, startling look, like an adult man. Her nose is perfectly formed, neat and noble. Her lip is long, as if it were stretched to close with difficulty over the front teeth. She wears no make-up, her lips are perfectly colorless, pale and a little chapped, and they are ususally held tight, pursed tightly shut. She has a firm, rounded chin. Her facial structure is strong, pensive, its features stern and symmetrical as a statue's, blank, neutral, withdrawn. Her face is attractive. But there is a blunt, neutral, sexless stillness to it, as if she were detached from it and somewhere else, uninterested. (152)

The face is, of course, no less coded than the foot of our first example.[1] We are used to intimately observed catalogues of features in literature. What is remarkable about the use of the tradition in this story is that Oates rarely employs her gaze in this exhaustive fashion. She sketches her characters by a brief mention of their hair color and then, typically, looks through their eyes at the closely observed world about them rather than into their eyes like a rapt admirer. The function of the sustained description here is keyed to the problematics of gender. The hair suggests the familiar associations of female sexuality; but although as a turbulent "cascade" it evokes abundant "nature," which usually signifies feminine sensuality, the suggestion of wiglike appearance quickly undercuts this automatic ascription. Perhaps Gretchen is neither natural nor sensual? In effect, this description invokes the literary code of femininity only to revoke it, a strategy immediately employed again in the next two sentences where the eyebrows are emphasized as dark and thick, a feature conventionally expressive of masculinity; and, in fact, the eyes, those symbolic windows to essence, return not the modest glance of a woman expected in this context but the provocative stare of "an adult man." Further, this contradiction of femininity is at least a partly willful undertaking of Gretchen herself. Such is the message of the mouth, which has deliberately refused the application of the cosmetic allure of color and is "pursed" in tight rejection. The cumulative effect of this manner of presentation is summarized in the climactic series of adjectives, "blunt, neutral, sexless." Gretchen's statuelike physiognomy, as Oates orchestrates its meaning, is a complex field of reference upon which is played out the repudiation of conventional femininity.

For Gretchen is, without doubt, an "anti-heroine." At thirteen years of age, her size-fourteeen body is evidently "graceless." She is a clear "misfit" in a "world apparently made for others," a world whose gender requirements are garishly evident in the people, objects, and decor of the shopping mall Gretchen visits in the story. Dodi's Boutique, for example, is resplendent in silver and black metallic strips. The idle salesgirls dressed in pants suits nod their blank and beautiful heads to the rock music piped into the store. Occasionally one of them inquires if she can be any help in an "indifferent, bright manner" (151).

Gretchen's actions in the story rebel against the alienating strictures of a system that would define her in terms—artificial, commercially attractive, thoughtlessly benign—that are appropriate to the stylized world of the salesgirl. In one store Gretchen shoplifts a tube of pale pink lipstick, "Spring Blossom," which she takes into the "Ladies Room" (150) to examine, destroy, and discard. As if to underscore her rejection, she also breaks the toilet into which she tosses the pilfered lipstick. And in Dodi's Boutique, Gretchen takes several dresses into the changing cubicle. She muddies one with her boots; she deliberately tears the zipper out of another.

What changes the focus of this story from Gretchen as a rebel-victim to Gretchen as a transgressive protagonist is the intriguing contest central to the action. Gretchen is not merely out shopping on a November Saturday afternoon; she is engaged in hunting down an imaginary antagonist who leads her from an open field into the mall, through several stores, and home again. "The Invisible Adversary" (147), a male figure, is the target of Gretchen's hostility throughout the story: *"You'll be sorry for that, you bastard"* (149). *"You'll regret this"* (151). *You'll get yours* (152). Gretchen's "stalking" maneuvers finally force the Adversary out onto the highway where he is struck by a car. He is "limping like an old man" (153) as they both return to Gretchen's home. The story ends with Gretchen watching television: "If the Adversary comes crawling behind her, groaning in pain, weeping, she won't even bother to glance at him" (154).

The sequence of events and attitudes demands that the reader determine who or what The Invisible Adversary represents and what his function is in the story. The thematic contest that engages Gretchen, we have already discovered, is the struggle for and against gender identity. Certainly this projection acts out a role in that struggle. In a 1979 review of a biography of Carl Jung, Oates indicates her extensive knowledge and admiration of Jungian theory, (reprinted. "Legendary Jung" 159–164), so perhaps we may identify the Adversary as an animus figure, that personification of the masculine component of a woman's unconscious typically projected in dreams and fantasies. The objective of Jungian therapy is the integration of all the unconscious elements of the personality, but what is most striking in Gretchen's story is the violence with which she strives to destroy and reject what Jung understood as her masculine nature.

The text suggests only two coded means to gender production, which do not appear to intersect. The woman may participate in the endless replication of the feminine body and her domestic accoutrements through purchase that is encoded in the capitalistic system and epitomized in the reiterated "family rooms" Gretchen sees displayed in her "ritual" browsing at the furniture store:

Again she notices the sofa that is like the sofa in their family room at home. . . . All over the store there are sofas, chairs, tables, beds. . . . People stroll around them, in and out of little displays, meant to be living rooms, dining rooms, bedrooms, family rooms . . . like seeing the inside of a hundred houses. (151)

Gretchen herself participates directly in the practice of a masculine code of aggression. When one of the boys clowning around in the mall bumps into her, pushing her against a trash can, the whole group laughs as someone yells, "Watch it, babe!" Enraged, Gretchen knocks over the can, spilling trash all over the sidewalk and forcing some women shoppers to scurry out of the way. That the seemingly desultory destructiveness is really constitutive is evident in the emphatic differentiation in this encounter between the powerful males and the victimized female "babe," and between the forceful Gretchen imitating the masculine mode and the flustered powerless women. Further, Gretchen's general anger and resultant vandalism are codified by the story as components of the ritualized stalking, hunting, and killing, activities of the primitive male hero. But Gretchen is not a hero, although it is her masculine capacity for anger and physical strength that compromises her participation in the feminine world "apparently made for others." In the same way that she has tried to feminize her large feet by stuffing them into the feminine white boots purchased by her mother only to finally react by damaging them when the transformation proved inadequate and incompatible, Gretchen responds with distressed ambivalence to the gender definitions of her shopping-center world. Rather than embracing her masculine capabilities to define herself as a rebel contradicting, negating restrictive feminine identification, Gretchen becomes a transgressor. Instead of claiming, like Ellison's "invisible man," some free but lunatic space outside the arena of constricting definition—the open field of the "Invisible Adversary" at the beginning of this story, for example—Gretchen compulsively enters and re-enters the mall where she is repeatedly attracted to its signifying objects.

She reaches for the lipstick and the dresses again and again, only to destroy them out of frustration at their lack of congruence with her own requirements. By fantasizing the destruction of her masculine capabilities, Gretchen reveals a maladaptive complicity with a code of feminine definition that will confine her to the characteristic but ineffective rage that her story presents.

"Stalking" illustrates the transgressive "spiral" that by repeatedly desecrating limitation exposes it to examination and interrogation. I define transgression in Oates' work as a violation of the boundaries of convention and designate Oates' target of transgression as the maladaptive restriction imposed by gender ideology that this story exemplifies.

PROGRESSION/REGRESSION/TRANSGRESSION

We will best understand the process of gender identification treated in Oates' family fiction through the intersection of social and psychological theories. In the last chapter we read Swan's murder of his ideological father in *A Garden of Earthly Delights* as an emphatic gesture of the refusal of capitalistic interpretations of power, but we may also discover in Swan's actions the outlines of a more familiar story: the Oedipus complex that Freud defined as "an emotional attachment of the child to the parent of the opposite sex accompanied by an attitude of rivalry to the parent of the same sex" ("The Resistance to Psycho-Analysis" 214). In the novel, Swan murders his father, and he is evidently attracted to his mother.[2]

When Swan is ten years old Clara takes him to visit some of Revere's relatives. The boring hours of dining and visiting are relieved for the boy by moments of confusing intimacy with his mother. While she showers Swan waits on her bed imagining what life would be like for the two of them if they did not return to Revere's home.

Clara came out barefoot, smoothing her slip over her thighs. She wore a black slip. Swan watched her and felt something warm in his blood like shells that seemed hard but became transparent and then dissolved away. (324)

Like the description of Gretchen's face in "Stalking," this scene must be read with reference to the narrative code it invokes as well as to the action it contains. Clara, high-spirited, attractive, and unheeding, seems unaware of her provocative effect, but a reader must recognize the elements of a scene of seduction: the woman bathing, the young male kept waiting, the black slip, the disarray of the hair, the physical invitation of "smoothing the slip over her thighs," the lack of restraint indicated by her bare feet, the bed.

The next afternoon, Swan and Clara visit a museum where they meet a man with whom they had dined on the previous evening. On the following day, Clara drops Swan off at the library where he waits for her for hours. Suspecting an assignation, he angrily whispers, "That bitch," under his breath (329). Years later, just before the murder-suicide at the conclusion of the book, Swan feels he must confess to a prostitute he once called his mother an ugly name.

In an 1897 letter to Fliess, Freud first mentioned the compelling drama of the oedipal situation:

I have found, in my own case too, falling in love with the mother and jealousy of the father, and I now regard it as a universal event of early childhood. . . . If that is so, we can understand the riveting power of *Oedipus Rex.* . . . The Greek legend seizes on a compulsion which everyone recognizes because he feels its existence within himself. Each member of the audience was once, in germ and phantasy, just such an Oedipus, and each one recoils in horror from the dream-fulfillment here transplanted in reality, with the whole quota of repression which separates his infantile state from his present one. (vol. I, 265)

At the conclusion of the oedipal period, the young boy, according to Freud, will have put behind him the "infantile state" of his passionate early attachment to enter his culture. In order to take his rightful place as an adult member of his father's gender, he must abandon the indiscriminate longings that have gradually crystalized around the first object of his love, his mother, and contain the impulse to eliminate any rival for her attention. The cultural imposition of the incest taboo to encourage this crucial "dissolution of the Oedipus complex" (Freud, "The Dissolution of the Oedipus Complex" 172) demonstrates that the oedipal transition is as much social and ideological as it is personal and psychological.

For Freud, this abandonment of oedipal orientation indicates progression, and retention of the illicit attraction after the age of about five years signals regression from which "one recoils in horror." I argue, however, that the preponderance of oedipal themes in Oates' work indicates neither progression nor regression, but transgression.

With these ideas in mind let us turn back to Swan's predicament. Swan's connection with his mother has been perverted through her capitalistic marriage to Revere much in the same way as his complicated feelings for her are subverted in the passage cited above by a code that semantically foregrounds a code of seduction in their presentation. It is when Clara marries Revere that she diverts Swan's affections to a scheme of deadly competition with his stepbrothers in order to secure for herself the power that her gendered position precludes, and it is the comparable distortion of love by economics that fuels Swan's angry reaction to the prostitute's reception of his confession. She has made no reply at all in response to his confession. And her very "blankness" in the face of what he considers "horror" makes him wish to punish her (366).

The crime demanding punishment is more serious than Clara's sexual betrayal. What is implicit in Revere's capitalistic family is explicit in prostitution: love turned into financial transaction is a "blank" that can absorb any "horror" because its conversion to economic exchange has stripped it of intrinsic value. Clara, a "bitch" like her semantic sister, the whore whom Swan addresses, has devalued his love. His angry words and violent actions reflect the confused attempt to reject a process in which he has willingly, if unwittingly, taken part.

Swan's story does not depict the depravity to which one might regress, as Freud interprets *Oedipus Rex* in his letter to Fliess. In fact, it is not primarily his sexual attraction to his mother, which is minimized in the novel, nor the murder of his father, which the story presents as almost accidental, that is most significant, but Swan's need to create through definitive gesture what his confession has failed to elicit—moral meaning rather than economic blankness. Paradoxically, it is in order to assert the necessity for moral distinction that *A Garden of Earthly Delights* at once invokes and transgresses the Freudian code. Swan's narrative provokes "horror" to call into question the use and purpose of gender relations within the family under capitalism.

THE SOCIAL COMPLEX

Our consideration of Swan's plight demonstrates that oedipal relations in Oates' fiction must be read to indicate cultural predicament as well as personal problem. As Juliet Mitchell observes in *Psychoanalysis and Feminism*: the "Oedipus complex is not a set of attitudes to other people, but a pattern of relationships between a set of places" ideologically predicated (64). According to Mitchell, Freudian theory describes the genesis of gender arrangements instituted through the oedipal transition, and, provided with this description, we must examine their suitability to present needs.

I want to propose that with the dissolution of the Oedipus complex man enters finally into his humanity (always a precarious business). But it seems that the definition of that humanity—the differentiating instance between man and beast, i.e. the development of exchange relationships, may have become 'unsuitable' for the particular form in which it is today expressed. Freud having shown us the heritage that we have access to only unconsciously, the next stage may be to see the importance of the contradictions between this heritage and the present way in which it is contained in the socially and ideologically reconstructed family. (380–381)

Oates' narratives of the oedipal conflicts of sons and daughters demonstrate the unsuitability of present-day family gender arrangements by promoting the examination of "contradictions." There is no doubt that Oates places her transgressive heroes and heroines, confused, resistant, right in the middle of an oedipal crisis. This much we have observed in their general refusal of the usual dissolution of the complex through identification, that is, conformity to the normative innocence or violence of the same-sex parents. Constituted ideologically at birth as "boys" and "girls," their characteristic refusals demonstrate that they wish to evade the next step, their restrictive constitution as men and women. But since Oates is careful to clarify her antiromanticism, this tendency cannot be dismissed as a nostalgic desire to return to childhood. Denied regression, averse to progression, Oates' youthful characters often avail themselves of transgression.

The transgressions in Oates' fictions we shall examine as "romantic love" and "incest" should be understood not as tales of indiscretion but as a discourse committed to the violation of taboos with the effect of interrogating patriarchal stricture, a conclusion supported by three observations. First, Oates shows no interest in incest per se. Her refusal of the brother-sister relationship considered in chapter 3 rejects what Luciano P. R. Santiago in *The Children of Oedipus* describes as its most predominant form. Second, the only actual instance of parent-child incest occurring in her works is treated as an illustration of depravity rather than an opportunity to explore what we are defining as transgressive interrogation. When Bert, the father of young Clara's best friend Rosalie in *A Garden of Earthly Delights*, is dragged out of his migrant worker's shack and murdered for sexually molesting his daughter, the witnessing Walpoles are terrified by the violent display of crude social force, but they are in accord with the principle of justice that determined Bert's fate (80–81). Finally, when Oates does make use of incestuous material, there is always mediating intervention to ensure its status as symbolic rather than actual. Themes of the unfulfilled "romantic" love of sons for their mothers are marked by tones of authorial derision, while the incestuous liaisons of the daughters always occur with figurative rather than biological fathers.

I emphasize the symbolic register of Oates' themes of incest because such an interpretation contradicts previous critical opinion. Anne Z. Mickelson contends that oedipal conflict is the central theme of Joyce Carol Oates, whom she accuses of "working out her own fears and obsessions through the medium of fiction" (15–34), and Cynthia Charlotte Stevens argues that despite the ostensible social and economic variety presented in Oates' fiction, all her works are, in fact, organized around a central "Freudian premise that all children find themselves . . . confronted by their shameful and guilt-producing attachment to the parent of the opposite sex" (5), that "unlike the 'so-called' normal individual," Oates' characters regress to an "earlier stage of analsadistic sexuality" (6), and that as a result of the "fatalistically determining" (2) family relationships her fiction presents, any re-examination of the definitions of *masculine* and *feminine* from a feminist perspective is doomed to failure "because of every individual's unchangeable psycho-sexual orientation" (4).

In my view, the role of the family as it intersects with society is crucial in Oates' fiction, and a central instance of this intersection is the family constellation Freud described as oedipal, but in Oates' treatment this instance introduces the interrogation of sex roles rather than the ascription of the fatality of gender. It is from this perspective that we shall examine, in this chapter, the "romantic" boy as he appears in *Expensive People*, *Wonderland*, and *them*, and, in the next, the "incestuous" girls of *With Shuddering Fall*, "The Molesters," "Childhood," *Do with Me What You Will*, *them*, *Childwold*, and *Angel of Light*.

NOBLEMEN IN EXILE

"But, Richard, you should understand that it's always an awkward situation. Having a mother, I mean. . . . You're very fortunate. Your mother is young and beautiful, and you must know that most of our mothers, the mothers of the kids at school, are sort of getting along. My mother is at that age now, you know, where I have to watch out for her."

"How?"

"Oh, tag along like this, eavesdrop, make sure she doesn't lose something or burst into tears." (*Expensive People* 59–60)

This gallant speech by one ten-year-old boy to another illustrates the quality of courtly romance as Oates presents it. For Denis de Rougemont the tradition that Oates parodies derives from "but a single theme—love; and not a happy, crowned and satisfied love . . . but on the contrary love perpetually unsatisfied—and but two characters: a poet reiterating his plaint eight hundred, nine hundred, a thousand times; and a fair lady who ever says 'No' "(75).[3]

Richard of the above passage is the plaintive knight of *Expensive People*; his mother, whom he calls "Nada," is the frigid queen. In *Oedipus Rex* the confrontation between son and father initiates the drama; in Oates' novel, as in the courtly convention, the King is suppressed, restricting the focus to the mother's inaccessible love and the son's frantic isolation. Richard's postmodern confession is also a parody of the reiteration characteristic of de Rougemont's troubadour. Richard explains that he postponed starting his memoir, but once begun, a "kind of quiet, blubbering hysteria has set in" that may last "forever" (5).

The tradition of courtly love demands, according to C. S. Lewis in *The Allegory of Love*, the practice of humility, courtesy, a chaste adultery, and a religion of love patterned on the vassalage of feudalism (2). Reserving for Jesse of *Wonderland* and Jules of *them* the illustration of Oates' treatments of religion and knightly service, Richard of *Expensive People* exemplifies the first three aspects.

As he presents himself, "not interesting . . . runty and worried, an old man already," Richard, love-sick as a little boy and manic as a matricidal teenager, demonstrates the requisite "humility" of a romantic suitor. But maladroit Richard, that "damned, doomed child" (11), is not so much a character as a perspective from which to examine the implications of an oedipal transition that can bring him to the brink of maturity while denying him the maternal nurturance he deems central to his development.

Whereas the troubadours who celebrated courtly love emphasized the nobility of the knight's self-sacrifice, Oates' passage hints at other motives of the romantic son. The humorous reversal of his strategies for "taking care of" the childish mother imaginatively secures for the son the experience of the control that is usually her prerogative and projects upon her the maternal attention he himself desires.

Richard's *leys d'amor*, the courtly code of "courtesy" (de Rougemont 75), is that of a polite child on exhibition at an adult party, but his steadfast "please's" and "thank you's" are not so much a display of honor to his lady as a means of her control. As in the initial passage, where the speaker's respectful manner masks his manipulative eavesdropping, Richard's politeness obscures his predominant activity—spying on his mother. It is in this activity that Richard believes he truly excels: he was a "genius" in creating "devices for spying" (82). It is through this covert penetration of his mother's privacy that Richard fulfills the terms of the oxymoronic "chaste adultery" of the knight's code. For Nada lives a kind of split. She is both a suburban wife and a prominent "minor" author (17). Richard, however, is the child of Nada's external situation; both he and his father are denied entrance into her internal life: Nada forbids both Richard and his father to read her writing, and both are barred from her study. When Richard listens to her arguments, his "head stuck inside the laundry-chute" (82), and pries into her published writing and her personal files, he acts out a kind of asexual rape of his mother's separate and secret self.

Richard himself conceives of his affection for his mother in the vocabulary of chivalric romance, the rhetoric of courtly love:

We who love hopelessly are like noblemen in exile. . . . Our beloved exists within the perfect halo of her own consciousness, selfish and adored, protected by the very violence of the love we feel. Is this a boy's love for his mother, you're wondering? Eh? (183)

Although he admits his nobleman posture is really "sentimental bombast," he does insist that there is a "kingdom" of maternal love he aspires to create with Nada (183).

Two means into that imaginary "kingdom" are featured in the novel. Richard, like any knight-errant, attempts to subdue a dragon to gain his lady's favor. When that effort does not avail he turns to the ritual of *donnai*—the poetic recitation of his lady's praise (de Rougemont 76). The terrifying mythological creature that Richard attempts to slay is, in its modern guise, the "behemoth" in the name Johns Behemoth, an exclusive preparatory school for which Nada insists Richard qualify. "[L]ook intelligent. Don't fail me," Nada whispers before Richard's interview. He is her champion, and his field of honor is the rigorous written test he must pass to gain admission to the prestigious academy. Richard fights his way through "verbal skills," and "achievement" (46) and struggles through "Attitudinal Testing" ("Which would you rather do? 1) Hit your mother 2) Hit your father 3) Burn down your house 4) Eat a worm). He throws up "what remained" of his breakfast but keeps on "bravely," feeling all the while "as if I were trying to fly with wings soaked in sweat, feathers torn and ragged" (48) with Nada riding on his back.

Although Richard does pass the test to attend the school, it is apparent that his championship is inadequate. To his extreme dismay, his mother insists that he beard the beastly exam again because she is not quite satisfied with his IQ score. When Richard fails to satisfy Nada in her external life—competitive suburban Fernwood, where a son's intellectual prowess is, like her furnishings, her friends, and her wardrobe, an index of a mother's status—he turns to the internal world of her fiction. Richard's memoir is a twofold attempt to win Nada's favor. First, it is a traditional recitation of homage to her. He calls her "intelligent," "imaginative," and "beautiful," "what most American women would like to be" (92). But more important, it allows Richard, unsuccessful as the child of Nada's actuality, to assume the role of the esteemed offspring of her imagination.

Disturbed by one of Nada's periodic abandonments, Richard penetrates the forbidden sanctuary of her study, where he reads several jotted suggestions for plots. One note calls for "senseless manic behavior in some natural setting...woods, flower bed" (117). Richard duly experiences a "mad spell in the flower bed" (217) of the Cedar Grove Bank, where he is overcome by an "overpowering fury." Stomping the pansies and snapdragons, kicking, biting, and scratching the "tiny faces" of the flowers, Richard feels a "holy strength that was not truly mine" (218). And, indeed, the "strength" is something he has expropriated from his mother's imaginative conception.

Similarly, Richard develops two more proposed plots. Nada has noted "the thread of a story" whose events are still unclear, that will conclude in the climactic "death of X" (116) and has sketched the idea "for a short novel" about a young man who secretly buys a gun and uses it to "frighten people" until the fourth repetition of this behavior when the result is a murder that he has been planning all along even if he cannot acknowledge it: "'The Sniper.' I'll think of a theme later" (117). Richard buys a mail-order rifle through a comic book, and proceeds to follow his mother's outline step by step. As in the flower-bed episode, he acquires an uncanny vitality along with his borrowed identity. In *Expensive People*, the full account of the climactic "death of X," Richard formulates those elusive events, such as the failure of his championship and the abandonment by his lady that lead up to the son's fictive murder of his mother in the sniper's surprising fourth attack. The mother—Mrs. Elwood Everett, a.k.a. Nadia Romanov the writer, b. Nancy Romanow in Tonawanda, NY—is, as her series of conflicting identities suggests, intentionally and radically unknown, an X.

Rather than murdering the intrusive father, like Oedipus, Richard attempts to kill off Nada's fragmentary selves to fix her in the single role of mother. His dream-kingdom is the impossible static symbiosis of mother and child that Nada—as her nickname, that satiric echo of Mama implies—emphatically rejects. I don't want to be called *Mother*, she explains: "No *Mother* no *Son*" (188). But if Richard's attempt to fix Nada into a maternal role is unsatisfying, he is more successful in establishing a father. Until this point in the novel, Richard perceives Elwood Everett as a peripheral and bumbling "Daddy," but as Nada rightly insists, he doesn't really know his father. Richard's murder of his mother is the induction into the violent order that empowers this unknown figure who definitively emerges only after this event. "I've had enough of this lousy American father bit! I've had enough of smiling and gritting my teeth and taking it in the guts," Elwood exclaims, "and from now on things are going to be different": the familiar "forgiving *Daddy*" gives way to an unfamiliar "*Father* you are going to respect, buster, or get the hell out" (253).

Richard's actions are a response to a social situation dominated by relations of power rather than relations of nurturance. As an editor at a Fernwood cocktail party puts it, culture is founded on "competition and greed," and it is "terrified by love" (199). Richard's oedipal transgression, the courtly attachment to his mother, is understandable as a pathetic attempt to retain the possibility of love in a culture that denies it, but Richard's aspiration of service to his lady represents a sentimentalized yearning for the fully satisfying bond with the mother that never actually existed in preoedipal experience.[4] Richard's symbolic murder of his dream-mother signals his aquiescence to the definitive violence that supports the "Father" defined by Elwood's metamorphosis, but Richard's entrance into the masculine system that produces the Father also apparently kills off the possibility of love.

Unlike Richard, who seeks missing love through exclusive care of the mother, Jesse of *Wonderland* desires an intact family safe in the unquestioned authority of a benevolent despot of a father. Attempting to pattern himself on the very image of Karl Pedersen, his adoptive father, Jesse fears his sympathetic attraction to his adoptive mother may subvert the secure identification he requires, and he is right. When, desperately unhappy, a drunken Mrs. Pedersen passes out in the bathroom, it falls to Jesse to come to her aid. Her great naked body is a spectacle that fills him with awe and terror. He is horrified by her grotesque vulnerability but fatally drawn to her through genuine affection:

What an enormous body! Jesse saw that her breasts were swollen, yellowish bulbs of flesh, the nipples raw, a deep red, circled with rows of tiny goosepimples. . . . He stared, speechless. He could not move but stood alone in the doorway, unable to enter or to retreat. . . . The body was so large that Jesse felt it pull at him, tug at him. Come forward. He must come forward. He could not run away. An odor of sweat about her, an odor of dirt—the earth—a closed in smell of vomit and breath—as if she had been waiting there for years for him to discover her, in this private interior room with bathwater heavily scented and bluish.

"Mother—" Jesse cried.

. . . .She looked up at him. Jesse felt as if a veil had been ripped away from her face and from his own, that they were staring at each other openly, confronting one of the terrible secrets of the world. (157 –158)

In *Expensive People* Oates portrayed the pathetic absurdity of the oedipal situation. In this scene from *Wonderland* it is primitive force that predominates, underscored by strong visual, tactile, and olfactory imagery. No doubt, C. S. Lewis had nothing like this in mind when he referred to the religious aspects of the courtly tradition, but Oates' presentation of Mary Pedersen as literal earth mother here grants her the mesmerizing appeal of a pagan goddess, while her name connects her to the Catholic mother of Christ. Further, Mariolatry, of which this scene is Oates' transgressive version, has in common with courtly love, according to Julia Kristeva in "Stabat Mater" that "both Mary and the Lady were focal points of men's desires" and that "both were embodiments of an absolute authority that was all the more attractive because it seemed not to be subject to the severity of the father." And it is precisely when the preemptive order of the father's language is eluded, Kristeva argues, that "the spectrum of auditory, tactile, and visual memory" holds seductive sway (106, 111).

In Freud's account in "Some Psychical Consequences of the Anatomical Distinction Between the Sexes," the son's incestuous longing for exclusive possession of the mother" is literally smashed to pieces by the shock of threatened castration" (257). Unlike Richard, who remained ignorant of his father's violent potential through most of the novel, Jesse has already experienced the threat of symbolic castration. Early in *Wonderland* his actual father murdered his whole family, wounding Jesse, who managed to escape. The murderous violence of his birth father has taught him the deadly primacy of paternal power, and Jesse wishes only to insert himself within its protection when his stunning apprehension of the primal mother plunges him into the incestuous abyss of preoedipal attachment. The oedipal dilemma Jesse has tried to elude is written large on the gross body of Mrs. Pedersen.

When she later pleads to ride along with him on a short trip to Buffalo, Jesse finds himself her reluctant protector in a comic escape that amounts to an abduction of the mother in defiance of the father. Clutching shopping bags hastily stuffed with hair pins and cold cream, Mary astounds Jesse with the news that she is leaving Dr. Pedersen. "It's a question of survival. My sanity" (164), she explains. But Pedersen's damage has been done: the sanity of both mother and son is doubtful throughout the episode. Longing only to avoid Mary's demands, Jesse nevertheless repeatedly agrees to "help" her (165). So the two of them, "a huge drunken woman and a huge boy, waddling along in the sunlight, both of them panicked" (166) register in a hotel and begin to eat huge quantities of food to fortify themselves against the father's impending wrath. Unfortunately, in her inebriated confusion Mrs. Pedersen has forgotten to pack many of the things she considers essential to her new life, so despite his "terror" of "being excluded from the family of men," (173) Jesse must twice drive back home for suitcases full of dresses and shoes that Mary deems necessary. And it also falls to Jesse to directly and repeatedly defy his father by slamming down the receiver or yelling "Leave us alone" (179) when Pedersen telephones the hotel room. "Thank God for you, Jesse. You're all I have now"(178) Mary quavers, but by the end of the day, when she has capitulated and returned to the family, it is her reluctant champion Jesse who is lost and alone.

Whereas Richard cultivates the role of courtly lover, and Jesse wishes to evade it, Jules "falls into" it with all the romantic abandon promoted by melodrama and popular fiction. Richard Everett and Jesse Pedersen experience their idealized connection with wealthy mothers in terms of plenitude; each expresses his longing for maternal nurturance through voracious consumption of food. Jesse's longing for love is, as we noted in the last chapter, experienced as enormous appetite, and corpulent Richard includes in the narrative of his emotionally starved childhood digressions on gluttony and catalogues of favorite dishes (31–32, 227, 255). But Jules Wendall of *them*, who grows up in poverty, does not associate complete gratification of any kind with his own family. His dreams of satiation attach themselves to Nadine Greene, a young woman who represents wealth to him. When Jules drives his gangster-mentor Bernard Geffen out of the slums of Detroit down Lakeshore Drive into the wealthy suburb of Grosse Pointe, the diction reveals that he falls in love with the neighborhood: "a world of foliage and dark red brick . . . such sights went to his head" (229–230). He "felt his heart swell with . . . something intangible and lovely. . . . not just connected with money, but . . . its mysterious essence" (229). When Jules sees Bernard's sixteen-year-old niece, the daughter of this world, she becomes its embodiment, the focus of his true "love at first sight," and from that moment onward Jules devotes himself to serving the dream of fulfillment she symbolizes.

More passionate than puling Richard, more eager than cautious Jesse, romantic Jules is well-schooled in the tradition of love. His characteristic form of expression is kissing Nadine's hand, and he is enterprising as her vassal. When she tells him that she would like to run away to Mexico or to the Southwest, he takes her. When they are on the road and she says that she is hungry or that she wants to wash her hair, he gets her food or shampoo even if he has to mug someone in a restroom or break into a house to get the money to pay for it. Romantic Jules hears music when he thinks of this girl "he'd dreamed into being" (254, 267). He feels as if everything is "under an enchantment" (273), whereas unsentimental Nadine Greene, the object of his stylized affection, wonders, "Why is it always love, love, love? I never heard of anyone who talked about love so much, outside of books" (284).

Like that of Richard and Jesse, Jules' dream ends not in satisfaction but frustration. An emblem of fulfillment, Nadine is, however, unable to convey it—either as material wealth or sexual pleasure. Like *Expensive People*, *them* recounts the adventure of an errant knight and a frigid lady. During their flight to the Southwest, Nadine's "sad, evil vision of purity" will not allow her eager lover to penetrate her body, and despite his desperate passion, Jules is faithful to the courtly conventions of chaste love: "*if he loved her he would not hurt her*. . . . He could not contaminate her with his lust; she seemed to feel nothing" (275). But Jules' devoted knightly service does not even secure her loyalty. When he becomes sick in Texas, Nadine, no more capable of accommodating the fleshly needs of illness than she was of serving those of passion, simply abandons him. Years later, when he encounters her again, the two begin an actual affair, but despite their lovemaking, Nadine remains technically frigid: "He believed that she felt what he felt—locked in a desire for fusion, unity, but turned back rudely, baffled" (373).

Like the situation of the other courtly lovers—Richard and Nada and Jesse and Mary Pedersen—the physical disunion of Jules and Nadine (Nada's cognate counterpart) indicates the son's central problem: inevitable emotional isolation, extending from maternal to social relations. The fact of absolute separation is the most important shared feature of the three courtly narratives, each of which is motivated by the son's overriding need for connection.

It is this need that links Nadine to the mother figures of the other works. Musing about his obsessive love for her, Jules discovers its source in his own desire for the maternal "sympathy women drew up from the deepest, most private part of their beings." It is this capacity for "impersonal, blind compassion, almost a yearning for physical union, that he felt in Nadine though she hadn't the body of a mother or a sister but the body of a stranger" (336). In Oates' fiction, this "sympathy" is the ideal quality of the mother, and it stands opposite the father's overarching power.

THE ARGUMENT WITH OEDIPUS

The explicit oedipal themes of *Expensive People* and *Wonderland* and the implicit oedipal theme of *them* represent the desire for human connection, sympathetic understanding, imaginable as the nurturing connection to an idealized mother but impossible in the adult gender structure that decrees that in order for a boy to become a man he must "smash" the only nurturance he has encountered, however imperfectly, in order to enter a position of power supported by violence. Oates' narrative shift from the tragedy of *Oedipus Rex* to the comedy of courtly romance foregrounds the meaning of the loss of the mother in this transaction rather than privileging Freud's focus on the inevitable alignment with the father. Despite their evident discomfort, however, all of Oates' romantic sons complete their oedipal transitions, though not without registering through their courtly fantasies the nature of the restriction this transition imposes. The romantic loves of these transgressive sons symbolically violate the incest taboo to challenge the social order that debars them from the experience of plenitude, however imaginary. Oates' version of the son's predicament questions the appropriateness of gender arrangements that so strictly separate the attributes of nurturance and power.

Yet in spite of the plausibility of their motives, Oates consistently styles her courtly romantics in tones of mockery. Young Richard is a "wheezing reed"; "dutifully" awaiting his mother "behind thick glasses" (97); he is her mock-heroic "prodigy" (37), "her darling, her good genius" (75). His adolescent self, who recounts the story, is a fleshy "bulk," conscious of himself as the butt of humor: "you would smile to hear me talk thusly. Such a poor and pimply boy, and only eighteen" (84). Also grotesquely obese, when Jesse is abandoned by the Pedersens he consoles himself at a diner, where despite our pity, the readers' point of view gravitates to that of the sailors and waitress who observe his desperate and degrading consumption:

He finished one hamburger and picked up another. . . . he stuffed his mouth. Somehow the bun slipped out of his hand and fell onto the edge of the counter, and before he could catch it, it fell onto the floor. He stooped, grunting, and picked it up. He brushed it off with a napkin and bit into it. He ordered another Coke and then remembered that he should have milk; so he ordered a glass of milk. Then he changed his mind and ordered a chocolate milkshake. He noticed the sailors watching him from the other end of the counter—their boyish, intent faces—and the waitress. (183)

And Oates qualifies any approbation of Jules' love story by describing it as an insane deviation from his more genuine concerns: "The real Jules, a cunning boy with a sweet look about him, was overcome by the sweat of the crazed Jules, a Jules in love" (256).

Oates relegates all forms of literary romanticism—including the son's participation in the forms of the medieval romance—to the passionate attachments of childhood that must be superseded by adult social arrangement. Her depictions of romantic sons, then, both imply an argument with Oedipus and signal its limits. Her distancing tone in these narratives, especially the repulsive orality of Richard and Jesse, precludes any nostalgic regression to childhood. Like Freud's, Oates' works endorse maturity. Her presentation of the romantic sons of *Expensive People*, *Wonderland*, and *them* exaggerates the pathos of the isolated son's unappeasable appetite for the nurturing human connection that his culture withholds —"All I ask," Richard explains, "is the strength to fill the emptiness inside me, to stuff it once and for all" (255). But in so doing she also calls into question the gender system that produces such desperate "hunger" as a necessary condition of masculine maturity. Oates' tone derides the solution that would retreat to imaginary solace rather than struggle to reformulate a humanized construct of power. It is this struggle that elicits Joyce Carol Oates' serious treatment of the oedipal transgressions of her incestuous girls.

Chapter Six

Transgression II:
Father-Daughter Incest

Although we have been able to make use of a definitive formulation of the masculine Oedipus complex, there has never been a like consensus with regard to the feminine oedipal pattern. This chapter will trace some of the permutations of Oates' transgressive model of this crucial transition, with reference to the theories of Nancy Chodorow, Maria Ramas, and Jacques Lacan, as it has evolved in key short stories and novels. The symbolic incest of fathers and daughters, a central motif in "The Molesters" and "Childhood" and in *With Shuddering Fall*, *Do with Me What You Will*, *them*, *Childwold*, and *Angel of Light*, addresses a primary concern of Oates' fiction—the daughter's struggle against her social restriction to powerlessness.

Freud's initial assumption was that the girl's development ran parallel to that of the boy: that locked in deadly rivalry with her mother, she longed for exclusive possession of her father. This hypothesis, called the "Electra Complex" by Jung, which Freud himself eventually rejected,[1] forms the basis for Cynthia Stevens' readings of Oates' early texts. *With Shuddering Fall*, for example, is used to illustrate "the typical ways which a 'normal' father-daughter relationship may develop into a distinctly 'abnormal' one" (32). Because Karen Herz' mother is dead, she enjoys a favored position in her father's affections as "his littlest girl" (*With Shuddering Fall* 163). According to Stevens, Karen must struggle to maintain this childish relation despite her growing maturity in order to "repress" the "illicit desire and sense of guilt" resulting from "the decidely seductive nature of her fantasy life with her father" (33). The direct result of this process is the death of Karen's lover, Shar, who is sacrificed to Karen's need for "her still-omnipotent father's 'absolution' for all her unconscious sexual crimes" (36), and the general effect of this process in all of Oates' fiction is an evasion of genital sexuality that leads to a repression of the feminine processes, "which seem uncontrollably fated to bring blood, birth and destruction" (7).

But Stevens is wrong. Karen does not evade oedipal attraction. The pact with Mr. Herz analyzed in Chapter 1 is a symbolic incestuous bond, and Karen is Oates' first full-blown transgressive protagonist. Having surmised her own gendered powerlessness, Karen seeks to retain her father's protection as a means of dealing with it; what she discovers instead is her father's actual vulnerability beneath the mask of patriarchal authority. Rather than indicating the deathliness of an inevitable female vicious cycle, the deaths in *With Shuddering Fall* demonstrate that evading the oedipal transition will not solve the problem of powerlessness. And although the pact in this first novel does not provide a solution to the central problem of the protagonist, it does introduce the principle of the distribution of power as the motivating feature in Oates' further presentations of the feminine oedipal situation.

The defect in Stevens' analysis is her failure to consider the social meaning of the oedipal moment. Based on the Freudian assumption that there are certain unconscious wishes that, tidied up by the secondary censor, find obsessive expression as fiction precisely because they remain unexamined, Stevens posits incestuous desire as the unacknowledged impetus of Oates' oeuvre. Essentially, this is psychoanalysis of the author. Literary analysis of the texts, however, uncovers in Oates' emphatic transgressions of the oedipal theme an examination of its operation that moves beyond psychological and biological determinism to social interrogation. Indeed, it is the necessary inclusion of such social interpretation that distinguishes Oates' treatment of symbolic incest in "The Molesters," the short story included in *Expensive People*, her second novel.

Attributed to Natasha Romanov in the novel, but appearing as Oates' own work the same year the novel was published,[2] the story concerns an ambiguous sexual encounter between a six-year-old white girl and a black fisherman. This core incident is recounted three times as the child's perception of her experience gradually expands to include interpretations learned from her parents and their social context. The first section is characterized by the little girl's short statements of direct observation, visual and sensory experience, and unmediated social response: *"I climb up into the lilac tree. The first branch is hard to hold. The birds fly away.*

The doll is back there, by the steps. . . . I never remember it or think about it until I see it lying somewhere, then I pick it up and hug it" (162).

Significantly, in this first version, although the child's awareness includes the color of the fisherman's skin, the information does not result in a racial label; nor does the man's touch—he helps her rub the "*dirt*" (167) off her body—generate a sexual description. This section captures the period before social interpretations are internalized; even the doll is defined phenomenologically without gender: "*It has no clothes and is scuffed. It is neither a boy nor a girl; its hair was pulled off; its body is smooth and its eyes staring as if they saw something that frightened them*" (161).

Motivated by the need for a sense of independence, the child has solicited her busy mother's permission to play at the nearby "*crick*" without supervision. (*"When I was little. . . . Mommy wouldn't let me come down. . . . Now I can come down by myself, alone. I am getting big*" [164]). She is aware of three interdictions regarding these visits, each of which she violates in an effort to experience her own developing autonomy: she is not to get wet; she is not to get dirty; and if fishermen from the city arrive, she is to leave at once.

Like the first, the second version begins with the statement, "*I am six years old*" (169), but the speaking voice has attained a more sophisticated perspective, clearly influenced by her mother's reactions. Instead of the direct presentation of emotion and sensation, the second account emphasizes the perception of relationships. She recounts that at the time of the incident the family was living in the country because her father was still healthy enough to work, but later they must move to the city to live with her grandmother. She also records her resentment at exclusion from a "bike trip" organized by her older brother and his friends: "*Nobody cared about me; the boys call me baby if they are nice and push me away and tease me if they're bad*" (169). Very much aware of the disadvantage of being the youngest, the protagonist also becomes acutely aware in this section of the misfortune of being female.

Left out of her brother's games and ignored because of her mother's domestic chores, the little girl is attracted to the stranger in the first account because of the attention he pays her: "*Nobody ever sat and watched me so close. Nobody ever wanted me to walk in the water and would sit there to catch me if I tripped*" (168), but in the second account, which explores less her own acute reactions than the politics of her family relations, the little girl does not run away from the man, as instructed, because by staying she can "*make Mommy sorry*" (172).

The child's awareness of her mother featured throughout this section culminates in the mother's discovery of the daughter's transgression, and it is evidently her mother's reactions that have shaped the child's more sophisticated awareness. In this version, for example, the child identifies the stranger's race in maternal diction: *"Now I know what he is: a colored man."*[3] What she recalls about the encounter also has a clearly defined sexual content shaped by her mother's questions: *"He took your clothes off, didn't he?"* (177). More definitive than the man's tentative actions or the little girl's naive complicity is the mother's dramatic response. The mother begins to scream and flail about the kitchen, knocking canning jars off the table to smash on the floor. Horrified by her red-faced mother's hysterical reaction, the little girl understands that *"something terrible has happened and that everything is changed"* (177).

The third account is determined by the girl's father and the outside world. What has begun as a somewhat tender, if misunderstood, incident has become a general condition of the child's existence marked by repeated and terrifying nightmares: *"I can hear myself crying. My throat is sore. . . . What if they all come in . . . all those people again, to look at me? The doctor had something cold that touched me. I hated them all. I wanted to die"* (178).

The final version of the episode is definitely shaped by the father's diction and values: *"The nigger was caught and a state trooper that Daddy knows real well kicked him in the face. . . . He did something terrible, and what was terrible came onto me, like black tar you can't wash off"* (179).

Richard Everett, the protagonist of *Expensive People*, concludes upon reading his mother's story that in addition to the "rather gentle" molester by the creek, "we see that all the adults are 'molesters'" and that, in fact, the "business of adulthood" is at least "partly" the kind of molestation the story presents (180)—not so much violation of body as modification of mind. By the end of the story the little girl is located within the predominant definitions of patriarchy: she is ineradicably "dirty" and the victim of a system that enforces its codes through violence. It is important to note that the fisherman appeals to the child by attempting to reverse her sullied condition and rejecting a relation of paternal violence. Through another version of the Oatesian device of the two fathers, he would negate the girl's definitive placement within patriarchal ideology. Children have two daddies in the city, he explains to her—one to work and the other to play. His concern and focused attention suggest an alternative to her own father's authoritative distance. Rubbing the dirt off her arm with his moistened finger, he asssures her *"I won't never spank no little girl of mine either,"*

and adds in contrast "You think they' d spank you at home for being dirty?"
(166).

Sexual transgression in Oates' works signals the conjunction of the fixed
social restriction of patriarchal culture and the ineffectual impulse to
escape such limitation. The daughter's oedipal transition often includes
incestuous desire, but the object of such longing is most often the dream-
daddy, as in this instance, who may offer developmental freedom rather
than the father who represents coercive constraint.

THE PASSAGE TO PATRIARCHY

The theories of object-relations psychologists bear on the social interpretation of the female Oedipus complex. Juliet Mitchell explains that
according to these theorists, "a sexual identity is first given biologically
and then developed and confirmed (or not) as the subject grows through
interaction with real objects and its fantasies of them" (*Feminine Sexuality*
Introduction I 12–13), a pattern apparent in the maturational focus of
Oates' family narratives. Born into ideological configurations predetermined by gender, her sons and daughters experience parents (or parent-
objects) and the fantasies those figures generate in the paradoxical struggle
to both attain and elude deleterious adulthood. Nancy Chodorow, also
influenced by object-relations theory, argues that it is the differing relations with mothers and fathers that effects the different gender contents of
boys and girls. The mother's role as primary caretaker creates for the boy
the distance that facilitates identification with the cultural definitions of
masculinity that Oates treats in her stories of sons, whereas the girl's
continuing attachment to the mother as central figure in her life encourages
the problems of separation and individuation outlined in our previous
consideration of mothers and daughters. As a result of this arrangement,
the father is cast for the daughter "in the position of the third term that
must break the asocial dyadic unit of mother and child" (Mitchell, *Feminine Sexuality* 23).

In Oates' short story "Childhood," which appeared in *Epoch* in 1967,
Thalia attempts to define herself in opposition to her powerfully attractive
mother Anna by enlisting Jake, a stepfather she has not seen in years, to
act the part of the triadic father. What we have defined as *innocence*—the
unquestioning acceptance of restrictive conditions—is Anna's most striking characteristic:

Never had a corner of her mind resisted. . . . Gradually all things—her father's
drunkenness, her first husband's cowlike weakness, the cancer that had killed her

mother, the drought that plagued everyone in late summer, the bitterness of winter, ants in the sugar bowl, toothaches, the long lethargy of having a baby, the finality of the grave that overtook everyone in time—all-blurred . . . everything blended to the same texture, so that Anna never condemned anything that was "the way life is." (215)

The disadvantage of such an approach is that all detrimental circum-stances—those that are products of social intervention, like "weakness" as well as uncontrollable events like "cancer"—are accepted as natural and inevitable. Thus, like Loretta of *them*, what Anna gains in optimism she sacrifices in autonomy. In contrast to her mother's blanket acceptance, Thalia is characterized by her general attitude of resistance. Where Anna is loquacious, Thalia is reticent; where Anna is direct, Thalia is evasive. In fact, it is just Jake's similar deviation from Anna's standard that draws Thalia's imagination to him in the first place:

There was no one's language that she could surrender to, really. Like her stepfather—she thought of him suddenly—at some picnic, a fireman's picnic years ago, when some friends of his had asked him to join a softball game and he had refused: he just couldn't do it, could not fit in with hilarity, did not have the grace that Anna possessed so richly. (213)

Thalia imagines that she and Jake can be "collaborators" (210) against her mother's overwhelming influence. When mother and daughter return on a visit to the hometown where Anna and Jake were husband and wife, Thalia sneaks to his house in the middle of the night to propose just such an alliance: "I've been waiting years to see you again and thinking about you," she explains ardently (211):

"I want to stay here again like before and I'm going to, I'm going to cook for you and clean up in here . . . and she wouldn't be here to wait for at night—That used to make me sick, how you would wait up for her in the kitchen. . . . I wished she was dead then!" "I wished she was dead too," Jake said. (221)

In this story Thalia sets up a classic oedipal triangle, but she is evidently motivated by a desire to separate herself from her mother and her mother's philosophical acceptance of powerlessness rather than by rivalry with her mother for the father's affections. So motivated, her incestuous overtures to a father figure are, as it occurs to both parties in this exchange, apparently not what they seem:

"I could come here and be with you," Thalia whispered. "I love you." But, as she said this, suddenly she was not sure of what she meant or to whom she was speaking. "In what way do you love me?" Jake said coldly. . . . "I'm not your father." (220)

Women's "romance" fiction, as Sally McNall defines it, depicts the daughter's problematic detachment from her preoedipal mother. To avoid the emotional turmoil and instability of the romance condition—"the terror and rage" resulting from "the girl child's inability to fully relinquish her unintegrated fantasy images of her earliest love, her mother" (120)— Oates' daughters deliberately seek transgressive relationships with father figures. The marriage of teenage Elena to middle-aged Marvin Howe in *Do with Me What You Will*, for instance, serves as a means to detach her "self" from the preoedipal "bad mother" projected as Ardis in the novel.

But Howe is more than a convenient third term to intervene between mother and daughter. He is the fictive embodiment of patriarchal power. As a successful criminal lawyer he has the authority to define actions and therefore regulate society. Everyone is "innocent," he explains, "until the crime he has committed is given a name" (99). "The law has nothing to do with history" (96): the power of law is the power to create alternative versions of experience. Marvin Howe, unlike Anna, does not have to accept eventualities as natural; by controlling their moral interpretation in the social context he can specify how human events will be experienced, not as abstract truth, but as concrete actuality. And as an outward sign of this ideological power, he has accrued the material benefits of his civilization, a warehouse full of worldly goods from the guilty clients whose antisocial behaviors he has named "innocent": furniture of all sorts, decorative accessories like silver candlesticks, "cigarette boxes made of delicate carved wood" and "a velvet-jewelry box heaped high with jewelry. . . . Marvin pulled a necklace out of this mess and put it around Elena's neck" (116).

This ceremonial bestowal indicates that by marrying Howe, Elena does more than separate herself from her mother; she also acquires something of Howe's masculine privilege, an acquisition that might be interpreted through Freud's explanation of the feminine oedipal resolution as the operation of "penis envy."[4] Becoming aware of her lack of this significant organ, the little girl is said to spurn in disappointment her initial attraction to her mother, turning to men to recoup her deprivation through the symbolic substitutions available in marriage and childbearing. Elena's subsequent actions—her separation from Howe and her struggle to gain personal autonomy—demand, however, a fuller explanation. Chodorow provides a more accurate account of the process in which Elena participates:

The penis, or phallus, is a symbol of power or omnipotence, whether you have one as a sexual organ (as a male) or as a sexual object (as her mother "possesses" her father's). A girl wants it for the powers it symbolizes and the freedom it promises from her previous sense of dependence, and not because it is inherently or obviously better to be masculine: "Basically, penis envy is the symbolic expression of another desire. Women do not wish to become men, but want to detach themselves from the mother and become complete autonomous *women.* (123)[5]

There is, however, a problem with this solution to the girl's oedipal predicament. According to María Ramas, the Oedipus complex

confronts the child not only with the sexual prohibitions of his or her culture, but also with the interconnected meanings of masculinity, femininity, and heterosexuality. Precisely at the "moment" that the girl confronts the demand that she turn from the mother to the father, the connections between activity, possession of the phallus, sadism, and masculinity, on the one hand, and passivity, castration, masochism, and femininity, on the other come into sharp focus. (86)

Therefore, "the Father and the phallus are *not* empty vessels that she [the daughter] can fill with whatever content she pleases—that is, with liberation" (82).

The incest theme in *them* substantiates Ramas' contention that at the oedipal "moment" the daughter must realize that her relations are socially defined as patriarchal and that this definition denies any projected "liberation by confronting the girl with new and seemingly more permanent forms of dependency" (82). Certainly this is Maureen Wendall's devastating experience. When she is fifteen years old her mother Loretta marries Pat Furlong, thus introducing a triadic stepfather into the mother-daughter dyad of *them.* This event corresponds with the developmental expectation that during "early puberty, a girl moves from her preoccupation with her relationship to her mother to a concern with her father and other males" (Chodorow 138). Maureen's development has been delayed, however, by her sensitive awareness of the disadvantages of both femininity and masculinity and is further complicated by her mother's instigation of a volatile oedipal situation.

Maureen both wants to grow up and is afraid of maturity. Concerned by her "failure to have dreamed her way out of childhood" (165), she is also reluctant to become a woman like her mother. "There were secrets of female life open to her, ready for her to learn, but she rejected them" (170). Maureen is "a woman, but in disguise as a child" because she "did not want to live with a man, sleep with a man. It made her angry to think of a future in which she waited in an apartment for a man to come back from whatever men did" (171). Visits to her grandmother in the nursing home make Maureen acutely aware of the fate of women: "bed after bed, aged woman after woman, all of them sisters in their soiled white nightgowns of flannel and their anxious, jealous eyes." In contrast to the "disinfectant-stinking," "stale" (166), and defeated "world of women" (167) is the overpowering masculinity represented by Furlong's physical presence: his coarse muscular body, "the graying, matted hair on his chest," his odor of "not just dirt and grime and grease but the personal, private smell of his body," and even the "brutal" sound of his breathing (161). Neither feminine entrapment nor masculine brutality offers much inducement to adulthood, but Loretta supplies the incitement for change.

Oates replied to psychologist Dale Boesky's question about Maureen's situation that he was correct in supposing that Loretta is "provoking" her daughter, "quite unconsciously, of course" into "promiscuous behaviour" in an attempt to "keep her husband at home. It is a roundabout kind of seduction, all the more sinister in that the daughter cannot even accuse the mother of anything, or even think, coherently about what is happening" ("Correspondence with Miss Joyce Carol Oates" 482).

As her marriage becomes shaky because of advancing pregnancy and Furlong's increasing absence and drunkenness, Loretta frequently retreats to Maureen's bed, forcing her daughter to minister to her husband in the middle of the night by serving his supper, making his coffee, absorbing his angry blows, and even providing the intimate service of rubbing his painful back.

As the compromising situation escalates, Maureen becomes increasingly more disturbed. At first she is merely confused—her excellent schoolwork deteriorates—but eventually she develops a protective numbness, "as if a shell were shaping itself out of her skin" (184) that allows her to pursue the only escape from her predicament that seems to occur to her—to acquire through prostitution the money that may enable her to leave home. Her clients are older men who are attracted to young, innocent girls, and when Furlong finds evidence of this activity he goes into a drunken rage. Although her sister Betty warns her to stay away, Maureen returns to the family apartment to undergo his brutal beating.

Oates herself stresses the incestuous nature of the bond between this daughter and stepfather: "it seems to me only natural that a girl of her age, in close confinement with a man, however physically unappealing (though in fact he isn't ugly—just rather coarse) might begin to associate him with her own sexual urges" ("Correspondence with Miss Joyce Carol Oates" 483). But it is with regard to Ramas' contention about the patriarchal meaning of the phallus that we must understand that the fitting consummation of this transgressive attachment is not intercourse but a scene of sadomasochistic violence that demonstrates that the girl may find in her relationship to the representative father not "liberation" from the mother's values, but the overwhelming evidence of her powerlessness within the patriarchal system.

INDUCTION INTO THE SYMBOLIC

For Ramas, the "Father and the phallus" represent the social meanings of patriarchy. Jacques Lacan accounts for the social effect of these terms through their participation in the order of language that supports and creates them. When the daughter turns from the mother during the oedipal transition she enters the linguistic system in which the phallus has been instituted as the privileged term signifying the power of the Father as it is established and experienced within the symbolic order.

What Oates' fiction presents as the uncomfortable "romance" world of mother and daughter, Lacan defines as the *imaginary order*: "a state in which there is no clear distinction between subject and object: no central self exists to set apart object from subject" (Selden 81). The contrasting *symbolic order* is the system of language that contains "the pre-given structure of social and sexual roles and relations which make up the family and society" (Eagleton 167). As we have observed of Karen Herz and Maureen Wendall, Oates' characters are universally repelled by the chaotic. It would be impossible for Oates' daughters to choose to remain with the undifferentiated confusion of the "imaginary" state rather than attempt to participate in the cultural organization of the "symbolic order." In her essay "The Myth of the Isolated Artist" Oates endorses a democratic concept of art based upon the communal possession of language and culture that "add up to civilization" (74). To be excluded from such community is anathema to Oates, yet this is the Lacanian situation of the preoedipal daughter.

It might not be unusual, Oates observed to Boesky, for young women to develop attractions toward the men they encounter, "teachers, ministers, older men generally":

Or it may be that a young girl . . . desires the appropriation of certain qualities in an older man—his freedom, evident wisdom, his knowledge and wider experience—rather than the man himself in any physical sense. My characters generally fall in love with people who will unlock a 'higher' self in them. . . .The love-object will determine development. (483)

The oedipal relation with the triadic father is attractive not only because it releases the daughter from the imaginary order of the preoedipal mother, but because it inducts her into the symbolic order that contains the discourse of civilization.

In *Childwold*, Fitz John Kasch's appeal to Laney Bartlett is precisely the access he provides to the "higher" order of the symbolic. He lends her books, takes her to museums. A philosopher, he symbolizes the patriarchal possession of thought articulated through language. Laney, an earthy teenager, stands, by contrast, for bountiful but chaotic nature. Kasch quotes Pascal: "*All our dignity consists, then, in thought. By it we must elevate ourselves*" (20). And Laney seems to be in need of some system—that of language and culture, "thought"—through which to organize, and thereby "dignify," her rich experience.

But there are, unfortunately, distinct disavantages to participation in the symbolic order, especially for the female. According to Lacan, by understanding "the function of the phallus," we can account for "the relations between the sexes":

Let us say that these relations will revolve around a being and a having which, because they refer to a signifier, the phallus, have the contradictory effect on the one hand of lending reality to that signifier, and on the other making unreal the relations to be signified. (83–84)

The transgressive relationship between Kirsten Halleck and Tony Di Piero in *Angel of Light* illustrates Lacan's pronouncement. When Kirsten is fourteen years old, believing that her mother Isabel is having an affair with Tony, a childhood companion of her father, she enters his apartment, searches through his possessions, steals the only personal items she can find—a few snapshots—and jumbles his neatly organized clothing and immaculate bed linen together with a can of toilet cleaner. Tony retaliates the following evening by administering unemotional physical abuse in Isabel's pool house. After painfully, but quietly, wrenching and twisting Kirsten's body, he runs "both hands over her" with no display of feeling. "He might have been stroking an animal, not to give it pleasure but to assert his own mastery" (142). Three years later Kirsten and Tony consummate this odd affair in a particularly dispassionate sexual encounter: "*Don't say a word*," he instructs her, undressing her "systematically" with "clinical" detachment (144).

These episodes reveal Tony's salient characteristics: the absence of personal reaction and the interdiction of human response. "He doesn't like anyone to be personal with him—anyone at all," Isabel explains (134).

Tony's stylized dissociation is also evident in his choice of art—"Anatomical studies" of body parts and corpses (132). Kirsten's initiation enjoins her to the same characteristics, but with one important difference. Her position in the sexual act is comparable to her situation in the pool house: Tony is active and powerful; Kirsten is passive and impotent.

Lacan states that the signifying process regulated by the phallus lends reality to the signifier while "making unreal the relations to be signified." Modish Tony Di Piero, who insists that his secret is "that I don't count," and whose essence, Isabel observes, is an effect of "surfaces" rather than "depths" (341), is a good example of phallic signification substantiated through participation in the signifying process rather than through accretion of experiential identity.

Tony's restriction against expression and response during sexual union may serve as a metaphor for Lacan's declaration that the patriarchal order makes "unreal the relations to be signified." In *The Subject of Semiotics* Kaja Silverman summarizes what in Oates' works becomes the daughter's Lacanian dilemma:

> there can be no resolution to the emotional extremes of the original narcissistic relationship so long as the subject remains within the imaginary order. That resolution comes only within the subject's access to language and its accommodation within the triangular configuration of the Oedipal paradigm. . . . However . . . these events result in additional self-losses, [which] alienate the subject from its own needs. (162)

The results of the daughter's entrance into the "unreality" of the symbolic order is the alienation from both the existential world and the phenomenal self. We have witnessed this "rupture" (Silverman 164) from the existential world in the protagonist of "The Molesters," who moves from initial phenomenological response to deepening abstraction. The second related loss is that of the phenomenal self. With her entrance into the system of language the female person becomes the feminine subject "split off or partitioned" from "its" own experience, sense of individuality, and "drives" to be "subordinated to a symbolic order that will henceforth entirely determine its identity and desires" (Silverman 172). Through the operation of linguistic difference, *she* loses her particularity to become *it*, the negative feminine term that supports the positive masculine term privileged by a signifying order in which the phallus is the determining feature. Through the oedipal transition, according to Lacan, both males and females enter the symbolic order and suffer the "losses" of self and world illustrated by Kirsten and Tony, but *he* acquires the prerogative of power and privilege, while *she* stands for lack and is formally restricted to powerlessness.

THE RULE THAT MAKES THE FAMILY

It is the role of the family to promote the induction of sons and daughters into the symbolic order: "The discourse of the family which is absolutely central to the perpetuation of the present phallocentric order needs subjects," and this "discourse of the family produces the subjects it needs by aligning them with the symbolic positions of 'father' and 'mother' " during the oedipal transition, Silverman explains (182). The thematic investment of Oates' texts is in the distortion of that discourse and the challenge to such alignments.

In order to achieve normative sexual orientation, the daughter must transfer her primary attraction from her mother to her father, but it is precisely at this point that the incest taboo against eroticism between parents and children intervenes. According to Talcott Parsons, father-daughter incest threatens both the family and society. The stability of the family may be affected by the challenge to the primary and legitimate bond of the mother and the father (26), and the social system suffers from any failure to promote exogamy through intermarriage, according to Claude Levi-Strauss. But the significant feature of the incest interdiction for our analysis is *"The fact of [its] being a rule. . . .* [I]t is intervention over and above anything else; even more exactly, it is *the* intervention" (Levi-Strauss, *Elementary Structures* 32).

For Oates' daughters, regression is unacceptable, and progression, although obviously necessary, is clearly detrimental. Like the sons, daughters do complete their oedipal transitions, but by practicing transgression through symbolic violation of the incest taboo, they illuminate the restrictions of the patriarchal order by breaking the rule that makes the family. Oates' works record the painful emotional actuality of the daughter's necessary insertion into the symbolic order, but by violating again and again the rule that initiates and defines that order, the daughter signals her resistance to the condition of that necessity: the formal imposition of impotence as the feminine situation.

Significantly, Oates entitles a chapter "Transgression" in *Angel of Light*. In it Nick Martens uses the word in describing his complex ongoing relationship with his father by recounting his equivocal defiance of his father's deepest expectations. I retain a similar emphasis on both complexity and defiance in my examination of transgression in Oates' texts. Underlying my use of the term is the assumption that a rule that is transgressed is not destroyed but merely violated. Such violation calls attention to the conditions that provoke defiance at the same time that it underscores their continuing existence. The repetition of this maneuver produces not reform but the possibility of reform. "Transgression," according to Foucault, "carries the limit right to the limit . . . ; transgression forces the limit to face the fact of its imminent disappearance" ("Preface to Transgression" 34).

Chapter Seven

The Feminist Unconscious

In this chapter we step back from the analytic description of patterns of refusal and transgression in Joyce Carol Oates' domestic fiction to consider the implication of such resistance as the struggle to achieve social revolution at the level of family experience, a project addressed in *Bellefleur* (1980), Oates' monumental saga of the American family, and *Marya: A Life* (1986), a biographical novel that organizes and extends the jolting feminine initiations and female struggles of previous works.

Oates' domestic fiction registers the psychological suffering of radically truncated characters confronting familial and societal environments that restrict them by gender to inadequate half-existences. The predominant pattern of refusals and transgressions by the sons and daughters of Oates' families demonstrates the centrality of both the defiance of limits and the desire for transformation of restrictions in her *oeuvre*, and the object of Oates' transformative vision is sketched at the very margins of her texts. The lost Edenic garden of the powerful-protective Father and the nurturant-empowered Mother of the mythic past is matched by the hypothetical utopian future in which similar figures reappear at the conclusions of some of her novels: the highly qualified endings of *Wonderland* and *Angel of Light*, for example, that tentatively introduce the reformed powerful-loving father.

In remarks to Dale Boesky, Oates provides an explanation for the interplay between resistance and utopian projection in her family narratives: "in my fiction I try to show that the local, the private, the family-determined, the political, the accidental, is to be transcended" ("Correpondence with Miss

Joyce Carol Oates" 484). In *them*, for example, she attempted to replace the restrictive values of the Wendalls with the enabling belief that "we are all members of a single family" ("Correspondence with Miss Joyce Carol Oates" 484). An important means of this transformation of the local and limiting family to the global and enabling family is the experience of what I define as the *feminist unconscious*.

In the preface she contributed to Linda Wagner's collection of critical essays on her works, Oates defined the purpose of the novel as that of exceeding restrictive forms of consciousness:

In theory a novel *is* this way, or that way: it celebrates the family, or attacks the family. . . . In theory. But in reality, in the existential unfolding of the work, it is always something else, something indefinable. That the writer labors to *discover* the secret essence of the novel is perhaps the writer's most baffling secret, about which he cannot speak, anymore than we are capable of speaking about the unconscious—the unconscious being precisely that which is never experienced by consciousness. (xii)

In an essay on Kafka, Oates defines the unconscious as "the undifferentiated primary paradise itself," in which "we cannot experience what is 'good' because 'good' and 'evil' are not yet separated into opposing forces; nor does human language exist, let alone habits of civilization" ("Kafka's Paradise" 272). In contrast to Freud, who taught that the social Ego must struggle to control and replace the presocial Id, Oates believes that incursions from the unconscious demonstrate the temporal, "local . . . family, determined, political, accidental" nature of confining and detrimental "habits of civilization." This realization is a first step in the imagination of reformation.

This chapter argues that the "undifferentiated primary paradise" of Oates' works is contained in a *feminist unconscious*: the repository for those forms and practices of humanity presently unavailable to consciousness that predate and exceed gender restriction. The empowered daughter, the loving son, the powerful and protective father, the forceful and loving mother—members of a reformed human family—are secrets Oates' fiction is trying to tell. This feminist unconscious of Joyce Carol Oates' fiction implies both a method and a content. The search for the lost mother in *Marya* provides an illustration of that content, whereas the narrative strategies of *Bellefleur* exemplify that method.

THE MISSING MOTHER

Convinced that "the Unconscious is wiser, older, more dangerous, more idiosyncratic, more generous, more therapeutic than the ego" ("Correspondence with Miss Joyce Carol Oates" 486), Oates' fiction develops characters whose resistance to the ideological formulas of "consciousness" demonstrates "a normal and desirable straining of a personality now outgrown or a social role too restrictive." "I am always concerned with the larger social/political/moral implications of my characters' experiences," Oates asserts, viewing the struggles and predicaments of these characters as representing the problems of "our society in miniature":

> the troubled people are precisely those who yearn for a higher life—those in whom life-form itself is stirring. . . . genuinely superior to the role in life, the social station, the economic level, the marriage, the job, the philosophical beliefs, etc. in which they find themselves. They must have liberation, room to grow in. ("Correspondence with Miss Joyce Carol Oates" 482)

The protagonist of *Marya* is such a figure. The refusals and transgressions of her development mark a representative struggle against a "social role too restrictive" that recapitulates the resistance to family interpretations of power central to all Oates' works, and the tentative ending of the novel suggests Oates' unconscious ideal of the reformed family.

Formally, *Marya: A Life* is a *Kunstlerroman*, the genre that traditionally traces the development of "a sensitive young man, artistically inclined," from childhood to maturity in his "struggle against the misunderstandings and bourgeois attitudes of his family, which is unsympathetic towards his creative desires" (Beckson and Ganz 104–105). In Oates' reimagination of the convention the protagonist is, instead, a tough and brilliant young woman; the struggle is against all forms of social and economic disadvantage, especially gender, that restrict female intellectual empowerment and artistic achievement. The novel traces Marya Knauer's growth from unhappy childhood to adult fame as a journalist to chronicle her own restriction and her active opposition to it.

Unlike *Childwold* and Oates' 1987 novel *You Must Remember This*, where the teenage daughter is left at the brink of adulthood, *Marya* tells the story of the years after she leaves her family for college, graduate school, and a career. This expanded biography allows Oates to augment the pattern of female development presented in earlier works. Marya's life recapitulates the three stages of the typical history of the Oates' daughter that I have outlined in Chapter 2 as first, the necessity of differentiating a self separate from the mother; second, the consciousness of rape as a cultural condition that implies the victimization of the female; and third, the attempt to counter the threat of violence through the discovery of forms of perception such as art, literature, or education that may balance order and vitality.

Marya opens when Vera Sanjek Knauer awakens her small daughter and younger sons for a hurried and frightening trip to town. Marya's father, a labor union leader, has been brutally murdered during a miners' strike, and Vera, who must identify the body, insists that her little girl look too: "Her name is Marya but she's the same as me—she knows everything I know" (12). But in spite of this equation merging mother and daughter, because Vera subsequently abandons her children to be raised by her husband's brother's family, the Canal-Road Knauers, young Marya is forced to develop a resilient and independent self. Less than adequately loved by her stepmother Wilma, Marya is autonomous early, because she has to be.

Marya's consciousness of rape, the second stage of the daughter's development, grows out of two episodes. Beginning when she is eight years old, Marya is regularly, if incompletely, molested by her twelve-year-old cousin Lee. Her only defense is stoic endurance; she cultivates the ability to go "into stone" (15) during these assaults. In the second episode[1] the resentment Marya has always suffered from her less intelligent classmates culminates on the eve of her departure for the University at Port Oriskany. At the farewell party given in her honor, several drunken boys grab Marya and force her to the muddy ground. "Going to Port Oriskany, huh? To college? Got a scholarship! I-got-a-scholarship! Ain't-I-hot-shit!" they taunt (128). She is strong enough to fight off their attempts at rape, but they do manage to hold her still long enough to cut off all of her waist-length hair.

In both episodes femininity is forcibly defined as victimization, and the penalty for asserting power to evade that fate is both actual violence and symbolic loss of the feminine identity symbolized by girls' hair. The novel charts Marya's growing awareness of the operation of the range of gender rules that confine her and her resistance to them. Obvious in the episodes of rape, restrictive gender ideology is also apparent in such simple acts as the way Lee drinks a bottle of Coke "in virtually one long swallow . . . a phenomenon less of thirst than of piggishness and stamina" (41), without leaving a taste for Marya who has been sent to fetch it, and in more complex encounters, like Marya's persecution by Sylvester, a janitor at the college where she has her first academic post. Although Sylvester, who is both a black man and a drunkard, enjoys limited social status himself, it is evident that the presence of a female professor is an insult to the masculine privilege he does claim. That Sylvester's displeasure is a matter of gender is apparent in the ways in which he subtly harasses Marya:

it was difficult to ignore Sylvester's taunts when he made it a point of passing her in the corridor, on the stairs, dipping his head in her direction in a parody of gallantry, twisting his mouth around the word "Professor" until it had never sounded so forlornly pretentious. And then she discovered one afternoon (how long had it been there? had any of her students noticed?) a bloodstained sanitary napkin placed innocently on the bottommost shelf on one of her bookcases. The thing had dried into a peculiar arched shape. (241)

In the third stage of development the daughter seeks a mentor to induct her into the paternal domain of language and culture where she attempts to master a symbolic system adequate to the expression of her experience. In contrast to Maureen Wendall of *them* and Laney Bartlett of *Childwold*, whose achievement of empowerment remains in doubt at the conclusion of the respective novels, Marya uses both refusal and transgression to achieve her goal.

As a result of her struggles with Sylvester, Marya articulates the distinction the pattern of refusals in her life also reveals: "She was no madonna . . . no somber *mater dolorosa* waiting inside a gilt frame to be adored; she was an Amazon of a sort, a warrior woman" (248). Whenever possible, tough, fractious Marya refuses the passive feminine role. She has refused a marriage proposal to pursue her academic opportunity, aware only of a strong desire "to get away; she wanted a room that so much belonged to her she could shut the door and no one would even know it was locked" (105). "Don't you start crying," her mother had warned at the beginning of the novel. "Once you get started you won't be able to stop" (5). But Marya rarely cries; instead of weakness and lack of control, she projects strength, determination, and resistance. This warrior-woman persona is best illustrated in the struggles of her undergraduate experience.

As a scholarship student, Marya achieves her academic excellence by extraordinary determination and demeaning small sacrifices as well as through native intelligence. She studies for hours and hours, and at one point she has to give up toothpaste to maintain her precarious financial balance. Marya's foil at Port Oriskany is careless and wealthy Imogene Skillman. Although dark-haired Marya is reclusive, even aloof, blond and demonstrative Imogene manages to lure her into a relationship. But in spite of the intensity of their friendship, Marya finally rejects Imogene's contrary qualities. Significantly, it is a sexual episode that separates them. When Imogene includes Marya on a double date and then insists that she wander around in the dark while Imogene indulges in a casual affair, Marya angrily marches back to campus, demonstrating her disapproval. Imogene retaliates by circulating degrading stories about Marya. However flamboyant, self-indulgent Imogene acquiesces to the feminine role; although she appears to challenge the expectations of her wealthy family and privileged fiancé through minor peccadilloes, she lacks Marya's courage and endurance in the attempt to define herself. Despite her sunny appearance Imogene is the "*mater dolorosa* waiting inside a gilt frame to be adored," whereas Marya retains the rigorous purity of the "warrior woman."

It is appropriate, then, that their final confrontation takes the form of a battle. Marya provokes Imogene by stealing an expensive pair of distinctive earrings, and when Imogene retaliates by grabbing the earrings and calling her a "hillbilly bitch," Marya strikes back:

What a sight, Imogene Skillman and Marya Knauer fighting, in front of the chapel, both in blue jeans, both livid with rage. Marya was shouting, "Don't you touch me! What do you mean by touching *me!*" She was the better fighter, crouching with her knees bent, like a man, swinging at Imogene, striking her on the jaw. Not a slap but an actual punch. Marya's fist is unerring. (182)

But to be a warrior woman in an Oates novel is not only to refuse gender restriction but to transgress it. For Marya the impulse toward rash and petty theft is a form of transgression: "a childish habit, she thought, disgusted, it wasn't even genuine theft, intelligently committed. Presumably she wanted to transgress" (137). This act has the effect, however, as it did in the earring episode, of compensating for an unfair allocation of power. Marya's theft of a pen from her religion professor demonstrates the application of this principle to the inequality experienced as gender.

Attracted by an interesting reading list, Marya signs up for a course actually defined by the instructor's intellectual simplicity and his expectation that the students show their amusement at his "jocular anecdotes." Whenever the professor alludes to "something female," he adds "as if off the cuff, a wry observation, meant not so much to be insulting as to be mildly teasing" (156). Marya makes the mistake of failing to laugh at these jokes. Instead of the A she is confident she has earned, she receives a C on her final exam and must go to the professor to "explain" her "offensive" classroom manner in order to secure the grade she deserves. While in his office, she pilfers his fountain pen: "The shame of having humbled herself before this ignorant man had been erased by the shame—what should have been shame—of theft" (158).

The principle of transgression as a means of securing equality operates, as well, in Marya's relationships with mentor figures throughout the novel. In her review, Mary Gordon notes, "Marya's life is marked by the presence of three rescuing men, all of whom die while she is involved with them" (7). Each of these men is a father figure. Each is already married (the first, Father Shearing, to the Church). Marya's relationship with each is symbolic incest, which, as I have defined it, is the transgression that violates female exclusion from the world of language and culture, and the recurrent pattern of the deaths of these figures supports the interpretation that Marya's motivation is personal empowerment rather than amorous association. Her compensatory "theft" in each case is of a particular aspect of the practice and purpose of knowledge, especially writing.

The first of these relationships is with Father Clifford Shearing, whom Marya loyally visits twice a week at St. Joseph's Hospital where he is dying of cancer. His existential Catholicism grants her a freedom that she had not been able to imagine: "In the high school everything female depended on being *pretty* or *not-pretty* . . . but God, being pure spirit, scorned to take notice of such trivial things" (75). Shearing is the author of theological essays printed in such journals as *Thomist Quarterly* and *American Metaphysics*, and as fifteen-year-old Marya transcribes his rhetorical deliberations for a final essay, she wonders if "to be able to write so well, to wield such a vocabulary; to *argue* so powerfully; to ferret out miscalculations in a rival's thesis to a mere hair's-breadth of a degree . . . if it is an entirely masculine skill, an art of combat by way of language, forever beyond *her*" (95).

On Marya's last visit, mistrusting doctrinal salvation, snatching at life, Shearing passionately grabs her hand. Marya is frightened by his transgression, but she misinterprets it as a violation of sexual rules rather than an abdication of faith: "Her immediate concern is simply for the opened door—what if somebody enters, what if they are seen. . . . She tells herself this is sin" (100). For Marya, the incident is consistent with the transgressive pattern of symbolic incest we have observed in Oates' works, in which through her passionate connection with a father figure the young girl secures for herself something of his gender-restricted power. The ending of the episode supports this interpretation. After Father Shearing's death the parish is surprised to learn that he has willed Marya Knauer an expensive Swiss watch. What "can *she* do with it?" people ask, "it's a man's watch" (100).

Father Shearing's gift of a man's watch symbolizes his sponsorship of Marya's access to the masculine intellectual world of language. Her "incestuous" love affair with Maximilian Fein, a graduate professor, is another step in the same process. The affair with the Mephistophelean Fein commences as the result of a transgressive signal that Marya is unwilling to observe conventional restrictions. After her admission to his special circle of admiring students, she is flattered to be bidden to look after Fein's house while he and his wife travel in Europe. On her first visit, after Marya has fed the household cats she gives in to her impulse to know the man by examining his possessions. "[F]ree, unobserved, a kind of bride" (198), she explores the contents of his library and even looks into his medicine cabinet. In the bottom drawer of the dresser in his bedroom she finds a brief note addressed to her:

> My dear brazen Marya—
> If you hold this in your hand, if you have ventured so far, I think it futile for us to keep up certain pretenses . . . do not be frightened . . . if I shortly make my claim. (201)

If Shearing represents the evasion of limitation through religion, the source of Fein's liberating power is more diabolic. His masterwork is a treatise on the advantages of perversity in Renaissance Europe, and periodically he feels "the need . . . to 'descend' once again into the depths of his own consciousness" (202). It is consciousness that is hell, he explains to Marya. Both of these father-lovers represent modes of liberation that Oates has explored. In *New Heaven, New Earth*, she declared her interest in mystical experience, which Shearing's childhood ordeal of near-drowning exemplifies (99). And Fein endorses the liberating potential of the unconscious I will discuss with reference to *Bellefleur*.

Marya's next symbolic father represents a third possibility. With the encouragement of Eric Nichols, the editor of a prestigious liberal journal, Marya gives up her academic post to become a political commentator. After his death, Marya finds herself at an international conference of politicians, artists, and intellectuals, hearing the same catalogue of political atrocities and rhetorical arguments that she has heard at other such gatherings—so much suffering reported to no effect.[2] Eric had considered himself a man with a mission, "a soldier in an undefined and undeclared war within the territorial boundary of the United States" (290), and although Marya had joined his ranks as a woman warrior against human oppression, she discovers at the conference that she has scrawled in her notebook: "Death from without & death from within" (273).

Mysticism, the cult of the unconscious, and political engagement, the modes of revolution *Marya* considers, are inadequate. Because of their insertion into a system of patriarchal values, all of Marya's relations with mentors have been marred by egotism, the mark of Oates' obsolete, romantic "I." Shearing secretly aspires to be *the* Savior; Fein is a self-centered, imperious lover who imposes feminine roles of worship and servitude; Eric's legacy, the "peace" conference, is revealed as the deadly competitive display of personal egos and national pride.

This inadequacy introduces a further necessary stage in the development of the Oates daughter. Restricted by gender to impotence, Marya has refused feminine innocence to acquire the powers of knowledge through language. Yet along with innocence, she has also rejected another trait restricted to women: nurturant love, the capacity to foster connection. As we have noted, her affairs do not end in union. Throughout the novel, Marya has attempted to deny gender in order to evade its limitations. The self-portraits she sketched as an undergraduate are forceful in feature, but unrecognizable: "Who is *that*? one of the girls on the floor once asked, staring at Marya's own image. Is it a man? a woman?" (134). And in her graduate period, Marya proudly described herself as "genderless" (191).

In all the earlier works of transgression and refusal, daughters struggle to resist and subvert the confinement of gender, but in *Marya* Oates presents the next step. In this work the protagonist has achieved a degree of empowerment by adopting a masculine militancy that allies her to the paradigm of the competitive "I." By so doing, however, the lonely woman warrior participates in a system Oates associates with external and internal death. Although Marya has had to forswear feminine nurturance for masculine power, at the conclusion of the novel she initiates the attempt toward wholeness by trying to reintroduce the feminine potential in the form of her lost mother.

Marya's mother frames the novel. In the first chapter she appears as "that Sanjek woman" who is for her daughter a confusing combination of weakness and strength, blurring rage and love:

She wasn't drunk because she didn't smell of drinking but she swayed and lurched on her feet, and when she zipped up her jacket a strand of hair caught in the zipper and she didn't notice—just left the zipper partway up. When she lifted the baby she grunted and staggered backward, as if his weight surprised her, and Marya thought, She's going to drop him and I will be blamed. (5–6)

Vera, is, of course, literally staggering at the news of her husband's death. Although young Marya does not have the understanding necessary to be able to resolve her confusion about her enigmatic mother, as Oates' readers, we are able to recognize Vera as one of a series of once powerful and nurturant earth mothers gone to seed in a hostile modern environment. Hugging her little daughter tight, Vera is wont to whisper, "You *do* love me—you're the same as me—*I* know you!" (8). Like other Oates daughters, Marya must at first define herself in contrast to her mother, but this novel also addresses her need to accept the potential mother in herself. While adopting Vera's protective anger, Marya has sought through her intellectual growth to avoid her mother's staggering helplessness, but because Vera has abandoned her children, the issue of the similarity of mother and daughter is postponed until the last chapter when Marya, facing the painful absence of nurturant connection in her own life, actively searches for her missing mother.

On the last page of the novel, Marya has received a letter from Vera containing the picture of a strong middle-aged woman with "Marya's own cheekbones and nose." Sensing that this communication "is going to change [her] life," Marya takes the slightly blurred photograph to the window, "holding the snapshot to the light, and stared and stared, waiting for the face to shift into perfect focus" (310). This ending implies the desirability of a renewed relationship of power and nurturance, without depicting its actual accomplishment.

If the first chapter of the novel invokes the mythic archetype of the strong and loving mother, the last suggests the utopian projection of the same figure. Like the powerful and nurturant father tentatively sketched at the very boundary of previous texts, this ideal figure exists beyond the experience of the actual family, although the ending predicts a reunion of mother and daughter. For Oates the full potential represented by the blended characteristics now restricted to opposing genders is not finally imagined as an androgynous individual but as relationships in the inclusive community of the reformed family.

THE SIMULTANEOUS UNIVERSE

Bellefleur is structured as a dialectic between consciousness and the unconscious in an effort to promote the development of the family as a reformed institution. At the level of manifest content it is a family saga that recounts the seven-generation story of the Bellefleurs in North America. Bellefleur, as the name of an American dynasty and its seemingly medieval manor, appears to represent a stable and inevitable order. Jean-Pierre, the founding father of the family, has written home from the American wilderness in the seventeenth century to define the values of that order:

There is only one principle here as elsewhere, but here it is naked & one cannot be deceived: the lust for acquisition: furs & timber: timber & furs: game: to snatch from this domain all it might yield greedy as men who have gone for days without eating suddenly ushered into a banquet hall & left to their own devices.

One stuffs oneself, it is a frenzy, the lust to lay hands on everything, to beat out others, for the others are enemies. (657)

Bellefleur is the family name for the ideology of the competitive "I," and the genre of the family saga implies the continuity and stability of family values. The pet project of the contemporary Bellefleurs, a complex scheme to repossess all the lands formerly included in Jean-Pierre's lost empire, implies such continuity, but the latent content of the novel actively subverts all stability and consistency.

Instead of the sequential history demanded by the generic saga, *Bellefleur* is written as an episodic collection of anecdotes that defy preemptive orders. If Jean-Pierre's statement of competitive greed stands for the limited and local Bellefleur family, Aunt Mathilde's quilt is the emblem for both the subversive style of the novel and the vision of enabling community the novel attempts to introduce:

Celestial Timepiece was the largest quilt, but Mathilde was sewing it for herself— it wasn't to be sold: up close it resembled a crazy quilt because it was asymmetrical, with squares that contrasted not only in color and design but in texture as well. "Feel this square, now feel this one," Mathilde said softly, taking Germaine's hand, "and now this one—do you see? Close your eyes." . . . Do you understand? (411)

Mathilde's quilt subverts and expands previous orders. Feminine and domestic rather than masculine and public, inclusive rather than exclusionary, it controverts the economic order of the Bellefleurs because it is not to be consumed as a commodity; it controverts their social order because it creates a cohesive system that is nonhierarchical in organization: no piece of the complex design assumes patriarchal prominence. Revolutionary, it enlarges the concept of the crazy quilt by adding the principle of asymmetrical texture to the existing principle of asymmetrical appearance. And the method of comprehension Mathilde counsels—closing the eyes to "see" with the fingers—parallels Oates' promotion of what I am defining as the feminist unconscious as a corrective to the limitations of Bellefleur consciousness.

The title of the quilt, "The Celestial Timepiece," introduces the central motif of this dialectic. Ostensibly a historical novel, *Bellefleur* repeatedly violates conventional definitions of time. The time-bound, historical, and local perspectives represented by the Bellefleur family are challenged by broader perspectives—sky-high in contrast to earth-bound. For example, whereas one member of a set of twins born to the family grows up and marries, the other retains the physical stature of a child of ten. Whereas the former is a "romantic heroine," the latter is a "child genius." Their divergent styles of maturation conform to the narratives that define them rather than to the practices of historical exposition. Instead of chronological development, the novel employs associative connection. Episodes from varying periods of Bellefleur history are interspersed throughout on the principle of thematic relation, and Oates' epigraph to *Bellefleur* from Heraclitus calls attention to her playful subversion of a primary category of determined order: "Time is a child playing draughts;/the kingship is in the hands of the child."

In the Afterward to *Mysteries of Winterthurn*, Oates argues that reimagining the forms of our perceptions "forces us inevitably to a radical re-visioning of the world" (514). For this purpose Oates favors forms that exceed the limits of conventional circumstances. In *Childwold* the grandfather is the source of stories that expand the experience of his auditors beyond the confinement of the actual:

Ghosts in the swamp, walking dead men with their throats streaming blood, the Death-Angel, gigantic snakes, bears, pumas, the strange-sized people who lived in the mountains....Grandpa Hurley drank rum and talked and talked, and some of the children left the table and went in the front room to play, and some stayed to listen. (172)

The unacknowledged imagination that informs *Bellefleur* is that of a similar spinner of tales, and we the readers are the children who linger to hear.

Kathryn Henkins describes the book as a "symbolic allegory of the American experience utilizing material from implausible events, supernatural creatures, mountain tales, in a patchwork structure" (292). But like Mathilde's quilt, *Bellefleur* employs a generic frame as a basis for a divergent concept of order. Oates' frame of the family-saga novel contains short chapters of fantastical tales linked together only because each touches on the lives of past or present members of the Bellefleur family, and this "patchwork structure" demonstrates that important sources of significance are available in associative contexts that would be omitted in forms dominated by the rational categories and linear presentation characteristic of the saga. Instead of the incremental progress of history, Oates' reimagination of genre foregrounds the sudden metamorphosis favored by the tale.

According to Oates, "[d]ivine legends; Gothic tales; childhood fantasies; moral parables cloaked in the form of science fiction, the super-natural, the mock-adventure"—forms included in *Bellefleur*—all create "wonderlands" that "share only their antipathy to the real or historical world." It is the shared function of these fictions to render "visions" somehow "tangible" and "tactile" ("Wonderlands" 487–488) like the diverse textures in the quilt to the second sight of Germaine's fingers. Especially, the "ruined castles" and "accursed houses" of gothic literature

are dimensions of the psyche given a luridly tangible form, in which unacknowledged (or rigorously suppressed) wishes are granted freedom. Impulse rises to the level of action: the unconscious is provoked—the unconscious "awakes"— what has long been buried seizes life and autonomy. ("Wonderlands" 490)

Like Poe's Usher, Bellefleur is the name not only of a family but of a gothic castle that suffers obliteration in the conclusion of the story. In formal terms, then, the gothic motifs of *Bellefleur* must be interpreted as giving lurid expression to the revolutionary overthrow of the limiting family by the liberating unconscious.

This dramatic shift from the quotidian to the unconscious is also urged by the reiterated instances of change in the multifaceted plot of the novel. Each of the various narratives comprising *Bellefleur* tells a single tale of surprising metamorphosis. A drowning rat becomes a magical cat; a husband turns into a brown bear; a religious hermit changes into a great horned owl; a brutal boy takes on the appearance of a mongrel dog; a silent lover transforms himself into the music of the clavichord he builds for his beloved; a child evaporates along with the pond he loves; and a dead man is made into a drum. Just as surprising are the psychological transfigurations: a transcendental poet who turns into a radical socialist, a mother who transforms herself into a business tycoon, a romantic hero who diminishes into "Old Skin and Bones," a violent sheriff who becomes a Christian, a hermit recast as a Bellefleur patriarch. The effect of the repetition of fantastical change is to reinforce the sense of revolutionary possibility: no order is inevitable.

The order represented by the Bellefleurs—hierarchical, competitive, and acquisitive—is foreshadowed in Oates' previous accounts of limiting families, the Pedersens of *Wonderland*, the Petries of *The Assassins*, and the Reveres of *A Garden of Earthly Delights*, but nowhere are the implications of their values so nakedly revealed as in the simple but mysterious tales of *Bellefleur*. The isolating pride and financial ambition of such families evidently produce violent extremes of domination: rape—Ewan and Gideon Bellefleur both violate Little Goldie, a child they acquire as the result of a poker game—and murder—Jean-Pierre II ends the

Bellefleur's labor dispute with striking fruit pickers by killing fifteen of their leaders with a hog-butchering knife.

This novel also graphically connects the values of the imperialistic family with the restrictions of gender. Germaine, the child who is the central character of *Bellefleur*, is born a hermaphrodite, a condition that may suggest to the reader the androgynous potential for full human experience, but to the Bellefleur women attending the birth she is a freak: "Just look at it! Shameless! You can see it's meant to be a girl but that other part sticking out—just look!—why those things are hanging half-way to its ankles" (145). Her grandmother acts swiftly to ensure the proper limits by surgically removing the offensive extraneous male genitalia: the "girl" is tailored by society to fit her gender—another Bellefleur problem solved with a carving knife! But just as the associative narratives of transmogrification through which the novel recounts the family history introduce another possibility—the diversity and mutuality of a new ideology of the cooperative "we"—the subversive countertext disputes restrictions by gender. Aggressive Leah, angry Della, the elusive Mrs. Rache in her man's trousers and leather flight helmet, passionate and impertinent Brown Lucy, Christabel, Yolande, Veronica, Violet, as well as Germaine herself, and the "headstrong" and "stubborn" (410) Aunt Mathilde, who maintains her financial independence from the Bellefleurs in a small cabin across the lake from the family estate—each of these women is defined in the diverse stories by her individual deviation from gender expectation. Bromwell, the young genius of the Bellefleur family, asks the appropriate questions: "What was sex? What were the sexes?" Having read of creatures in nature whose sexual function varied, he concludes that the significance of gender is as negligible as the Bellefleurs themselves in the celestial scheme of things: "the details of sex were of no significance, for wasn't life on this planet clearly a matter of . . . indefinable energy flowing violently through all things. . . . Why then take *Bellefleur* as central in nature? He much preferred the stars" (287).

It is also Bromwell who articulates the open question of alternative possibilities that structures the novel:

Might there be, Bromwell wonders aloud . . . a universe simultaneous with this universe in which a world like ours is propelled about its orbit. . . . Why not a dozen, three hundred, several thousand, several billion. . . . And might there not be, granted the identity of these innumerable worlds, a way of slipping from one to another. (290)

The inclusiveness of formal structure and the surprising metamorphoses of plot are affirmative answers to Bromwell's initial questions. Other orders are possible. The "way of slipping from one [universe] to another" in Oates' works is presented in *Bellefleur*, as elsewhere, in parables of conversion, of which the story of "The Room of Contamination" is a good illustration.

The most costly and elegant chamber of the Bellefleur castle, "The Turquoise Room" with its carved woods and gold-leaf ornamentation, was reserved for the family's most honored guests. One night before the Civil War, it had housed, however, three former slaves, members of John Brown's insurgent ragtag army. The Bellefleur family shared the common view that "the Negroes were the sons of Ham, and accursed," that the institution of slavery was consistent with the "hierarchy" God had established in heaven, and, even more pertinent, that slavery "answered the only important moral requirement that might be asked of an economic strategy: it worked" (251). So when Arthur Bellefleur, the "once-meek uncle" who had "become transformed—'converted' " (250) to the abolitionist cause demanded that his brother shelter Brown's escaping "soldiers," Raphael Bellefleur responded to his brother's ridiculous and audacious request with the sarcastic offer to entertain them in the splendid Turquoise Room. After Arthur's unexpected assent, subsequent guests reported strange "presences" (254), and when Raphael's son Samuel Bellefleur spent a night in the chamber to investigate these disturbing complaints he discovered in the great mirror, the crowning ornament of that royally appointed room, the image of a "mist-shrouded group of people, all of them black." The central figure of this company was a "black woman—a Negress—but not a slave," a mature, strong, and bold female who captivated Samuel. He began to spend hours, even days, away from his concerned family in the chamber that became known as "The Room of Contamination" after his total disappearance from the universe of Bellefleur Manor. Before that occurrence, Samuel himself had remarked on the divergence of orders the room introduced. When he discovered a discrepancy in accounts of the amount of time spent in the room—a matter of hours, he believed; a number of days, the family reported—he observed: "Time is clocks, not a clock. Not your clock" (259). And after Samuel vanished, the family permanently sealed off the infamous room for their own protection: "The room was not simply haunted, it was contaminated. To breathe its air was to risk madness and death and even dissolution" (246).

The Turquoise Room of Bellefleur Manor admits access to all that is excluded from Bellefleur consciousness. The family position is defined by Raphael's endorsement of Hobbesian social philosophy: "men require a common power to keep them in awe, for otherwise they will be plunged into war: *outright war.* (In secret, of course, they are locked in a perpetual though unacknowledged war, of which economic struggle is but one manifestation)" (248). Beyond the mirror of the Bellefleur ego in "The Room of Contamination" lies all that is disregarded by their political system: the black, the poor, the powerless, the female. And the sexual connection between Samuel and the Negress introduces love instead of economic control as a source of human awe. Samuel, who enters the mysterious chamber as the representative of a particular form of limited consciousness, is literally absorbed in the larger vision of the unconscious. The Bellefleurs are wise to fear "dissolution."

The story of the death of Great-Uncle Hiram makes it clear that the novel is especially concerned with the repression of a feminist unconscious. Throughout his life, Hiram, who is an acquisitive Bellefleur by day, enters by night the simultaneous universe of the unconscious as an habitual sleepwalker. Once, for example, Hiram awakened on the dangerous ice of thawing Lake Noir literally suspended over an alternative world:

he saw to his astonishment that there was a considerable crowd of reversed figures, some of them moving but most fixed in place, their feet against the thin crust of ice, their heads nearly lost in shadow. He wanted to cry aloud in terror: for who were they, these upside-down silent people, these doomed people, these strangers! *Who on earth were they and why did they dwell in the Bellefleur's private lake?* (648)[3]

Although the family lives in fear for Hiram's mortal safety, he never comes to harm during his somnambulist adventures. What kills him is a vicious attempt to suppress the female, which he associates with "certain" despised "bodily weaknesses" a woman "could not control, and were, indeed, part of being female" (650). Disgusted by the messy birth of a litter of kittens in his bed, Hiram imperiously banishes the mother and her offspring and orders that they be put to death as recompense for his "insufferable" violation. But spared by kinder Bellefleurs, the little family repeatedly returns to nest in Hiram's bed linen. Outraged by this intrusion, Hiram slams one of the delicate babies against the wall where "it struck with a surprising cracklike noise, and fell, dead, to the floor" (652). The protective mother, however, later retaliates with a small scratch on Hiram's chin, of which he dies a short time later. This parable of the death of Hiram Bellefleur suggests that there is salvation in the acceptance of the unconscious but grave danger in its aggressive repression.

For Brenda O. Daly the "Bellefleur manor is a trope for culture, a house erected on binary premises, a hierarchy of stories" (156). Consequently, when Gideon Bellefleur flies into it at the end of the novel with a plane full of explosives, destroying the house and all the family except Germaine, whom he has taken to visit her Aunt Mathilde, Oates symbolizes the dissolution of a philosophy of competitive power largely perpetuated by gender ideology within the family. A family is obliterated, but the ideal family as the institution of possible connection remains paradoxically intact in the final chapter of the novel that recounts the beginning of the recovery of the Bellefleurs after an earlier massacre.

THE FEMINIST UNCONSCIOUS

The feminist unconscious articulated in Oates' work, which I have illustrated with *Marya* and *Bellefleur*, is both a method and a content. We read in the ambiguous ending of the first novel the content Oates would like to discover in the feminist unconscious: a reformed family of loving and empowered members. We read the second novel as a narrative argument for forms that favor inclusivity and foster the imagination of metamorphosis by presenting conversions into the "simultaneous universes" that precede, surround, and occasionally overwhelm restricted patriarchal worlds.

For Oates, as for Fredric Jameson, the "recurring plot or theme in a writer's work" has "the analogous function of the recurring dream," an analogy she explained to Dale Boesky:

something demands to be raised to consciousness, to be comprehended by the ego, but for some reason the ego resists or refuses to understand. And so [the artist] is fated to dream and re-dream the same paradoxical problem, and he can't be freed of it until he solves it. ("Correspondence with Joyce Carol Oates" 482)

Oates' obsessive theme and plot is the American family and the misuse of power characteristic of all its social relations but most often registered psychologically in her works as limitation by gender.

Jameson adds to Oates' Freudian analogy the Althusserian concept of ideology, which accounts for the ego's failure to grasp the "paradoxical" and recurrent problem. For Jameson the *political unconscious* contains all "the collective denial or repression of underlying historical contradictions by human societies" (Dowling 114). Oates' more limited *feminist unconscious*, theorized as an anarchic region that predates social definition, contains that which contradicts all personal and public restriction experienced as gender.

It is the "unconscious" consistency of her work that is the source of Oates' literary accomplishment. Despite her expressed belief in the eventual reformation of American society,[4] Oates' fiction remains true to the articulation of present struggles. Conversions to the frightening liberation of the feminist unconscious are most often presented as formal resources of a textual dialectic that registers its own limits, and the utopian projections at the conclusions of her novels are tentative in the extreme.

"I try to write happy endings," Oates confided in an early interview with Linda Kuehl, "but they seem to turn out in a kind of green light I didn't imagine" ("An Interview with Joyce Carol Oates" 309). What Oates' endings have in common is the ambiguity of the implied future. In comments external to her texts, Oates may project her own optimism about her characters' chances, but the odd green light at the conclusions of Oates' family fiction confines the solutions of the problems it raises to the feminist unconscious, that revolutionary zone of the intersection of the restrictive and the possible. The potential of this alternative space, as well as its problems, is indicated in narratives of the "transgressive other," a limit figure analyzed in the concluding chapter.

Chapter Eight

The Transgressive Other

From the outset, critics have noted Oates' paradoxical treatment of the family. In a 1975 discussion of the early works Robert H. Fossum observed: "Repeatedly, Oates's people crave an order associated with 'home' and the loving protection of the father. Repeatedly, this conflicts with a yearning for the 'road' and freedom from the father" (49–50). In a similar vein Ellen Friedman remarks that despite "violent dislocations" Oates' characters are located within a family context; in fact, "it is a character's distance from 'home' . . . that is often a measure of the dangers that await him" (2–3).

Oates' protagonists also remark on the paradoxical repulsion and attraction at the center of family experience. Marion, of the 1970 short story "You," addresses her mother: "We fed ourselves daydreams of running away from you, slamming doors in your face, abandoning ship. Yet we will never leave you, you will never leave us, the relationship is permanent." "The family is the deepest mystery," Marion concludes, "deeper than love or death" (*The Wheel of Love* 329). Warren, the brother in the 1987 novel *You Must Remember This*, echoes her conclusion: "The blood ties are so powerful and deep and mute. Something terrifying there. How we feel about one another—even about the house on East Clinton Street— so strange, helpless, paralyzing and exciting both" (416).

What is the meaning of this overarching paradox? Oates' criticism endorses a paradigm shift from the competitive "I" to the collective and cooperative "we." In American culture, where the previously cooperative activities of work, art, and even recreation are increasingly defined by the competition of the marketplace, the only emotional experience of the "we" available, however imperfectly, may be the family connection.

In *The Liberal Imagination* Lionel Trilling described ideology as "the habit or the ritual of showing respect for certain formulas to which, for various reasons having to do with emotional safety, we have very strong ties of whose meaning and consequences in actuality we have no clear understanding" (277). The family as the site of ideological investment in Oates' works solicits inquiry, but as a singular space of "strong ties" in which to secure "emotional safety," it also operates in terms of ideological mystification to restrict inquisition.

Thus, the paradoxical motif of the attractive/repulsive family signals the bounds within which Oates' domestic fiction is inscribed. Jameson claims that the advantage of his Greimasian model is precisely the revelation of such boundaries: "it maps the limits of a specific ideological consciousness and marks the conceptual points beyond which that consciousness cannot go, and between which it is condemned to oscillate" (*The Political Unconscious* 47). The idealizations that frame Oates' domestic texts signal the outside limits of the consciousness determined by "family" as Oates presents it.

Oates' *oeuvre* is the presentation of American family as the classic dilemma of colloquial expression: you can't live with it, and you can't live without it. And, in addition to the fiction directly depicting the family, many of Oates' other works address the family-determined central opposition of power and nurture in the related institution of marriage and in religion and art. Certainly this is true in works that explore sex and love. In addition to *Marriages and Infidelities*, *Crossing the Border*, *Do with Me What You Will* and *Cybele*, books treating the terms of the couple bond, of the over 400 short stories Oates has published, according to Torborg Norman, the majority examine the intimate relationships of men and women (157). *Son of the Morning*, *The Assassins*, and *Angel of Light*, consider the possibility of the ideal synthesis of power and love in religious practice, and similar inquisitions of art occur in *The Assassins*, *Unholy Loves*, and *Solstice*.

The operation of narratives of refusal and transgression also serves to mark the boundaries of ideology within which Oates' domestic fiction is situated. We have considered numerous instances in which characters transgress the gender conventions upon which the dystopian family is structured, and we have observed Oates' subversive examination of genres and conventions—the popular romance, the courtly romance, the apocalyptic novel, the pastoral, the comedy, the tragedy, the *kunstlerroman*, and the family saga. Oates' interrogative use of literary formulas repeatedly inquires whether forms that traditionally serve the incompletion and isolation of the ideological family structure can be reformed to foster the radical development and connection of the reformed family.

But in addition to the dialectics *within* the text—the challenge of textual practice and the refusals and transgressions of family gender codes— Oates' *oeuvre* may also be understood with respect to its dialectic *with* the text, its superimposition of a narrative leveled against the text itself to decenter the social codes upon which it is organized. We have already observed this strategy in operation in the short story "Swamps." As noted in the introductory chapter, the murderous girl of this story attacks all the ideologies organizing the family: the role of the father, the proper behavior of mothers, the legitimating function of the institution, the "natural" bond of "love" expected to bind its members, as well as the gender expectations for her own sex. Another such figure is Arnold Friend in Oates' most frequently anthologized short story, "Where Are You Going, Where Have You Been?"

In the story, fifteen-year-old Connie is in the process of defining herself through a counterideology—made up of popular music, shopping center trinkets, and youthful sexuality—that contradicts the belief systems of her parents and her "plain" and "steady" twenty-four-year-old sister (*The Wheel of Love* 29). Mock-heroic Arnold Friend introduces her to the unapprehended corollary to heady independence: that in abandoning family norms she also loses family protection. Critics generally read the story as Connie's initiation into evil, and they discover in the ending of the story Connie's capitulation to the shallow values of a debased culture (Norman 168, Creighton 118, Wegs 92). In her own commentary on the story in a review of "Smooth Talk," the film based on it, Oates is also particularly concerned with the ending, specifically with the reversal in the movie version of the text's "unfilmable" last paragraph. In Joyce Chopra's adaptation, Connie is saved from the murder that is her probable fate after the conclusion of the story; in the film she returns to her family, "rejecting the 'trashy dreams' of her pop-teen culture" ("When Characters from the Page Are Made Flesh on the Screen" 22). In Oates' version, however, Connie does not return to her family nor abandon her puerile impetus toward freedom; although she will probably be raped and killed, as I noted in Chapter 2, the diction of light and open space of the final words of the story implies positive value in "the vast sunlit reaches of the land . . . Connie had never seen before and did not recognize except to know that she was going to it" (46).

That Arnold is a diabolic figure and a depraved lunatic is indisputable. As Oates reports, she based him on a "tabloid psychopath" whose "specialty was the seduction and occasional murder of teenage girls" (1), but that he is also somehow useful, even appealing, is the clear implication of the tone of the ending of the story. Arnold's positive function is that he openly confronts the codes of the family. Although he himself has no genuine identity—he borrows his artificial form from a humorous pastiche of teenage styles and slogans—he forces Connie into a recognition of the necessary displacement of the unexamined forms of "family":

The place where you come from ain't there any more, and where you had in mind is cancelled out. This place you are now—inside your daddy's house—is nothing but a cardboard box I can knock down any time. You know that and you always did know it. You hear me?" (44)

That Arnold has a positive function as the transgressive other to the text of the American family is demonstrated by the fact that similar figures of limit and challenge are a constant feature throughout Oates' *oeuvre*. Max, the manipulative esthete of *With Shuddering Fall* (1964); Richard Everett, the matricidal memoirist of *Expensive People* (1968); Trick Monk, the trickster foil of the protagonist in *Wonderland* (1971); Hugh Petrie, the nihilistic cartoonist of *The Assassins* (1975); Bobbie Gotteson, the "Maniac" of *The Triumph of the Spider Monkey* (1976); Fitz John Kasch, the post-romantic central consciousness of *Childwold* (1976); Alexis Kessler, the narcissistic composer of *Unholy Loves* (1979); Sheilah Trask, the "dark" opposite of Monica Jensen of *Solstice* (1985); Maximilian Fein, the demonic father-lover of *Marya* (1986) are key examples. What this variety of characters has in common is their contrapuntal relation to acceptable behaviors and communal standards.

THE FAMILY OTHER

This use of a "transgressive other" to the text as a projection of deviation—a struggle within the text against its own limits of consciousness—is a prominent feature of Oates' most recent fiction, in which the story and status of such an opposing figure are foregrounded. Three important works published in 1989 and 1990—*American Appetites*, *Soul/Mate*, and *Because It Is Bitter, and Because It Is My Heart*—mark the emergence of this narrative pattern and its related themes as Oates' central preoccupation at this time.

Soul/Mate is a revealing example of this tendency. Not only does the plot concern the actions and motivations of an extreme "other," a "psychopath" (163) in the tradition of Arnold Friend, but the genre of the work and even the designation of the author emphasize the thematics of "otherness." *Soul/Mate*, a "psychothriller" according to the book jacket, a genre Oates reserves for the consideration of the otherness themes of "identity, twins and doubling" (quoted by Wolfe 15), is the second of her novels to be published under the pseudonym Rosamond Smith. "I wanted a fresh reading I wanted to escape from my own identity," Oates explained (quoted by Wolfe 15), and in a discussion of Romain Gary's *nom de plume*, she posited the writer's need for "an erasure of the primary self," so that "another (hitherto undiscovered?) self may be released" ("Pseudonymous Selves" 385). This employment of an alternative authorial "other" strongly suggests the desire to test the ideological limits of "Joyce Carol Oates."

The structure and meaning of the novel also underscore this concern for the evasion of bounds. The two main characters of the work are Dorothea Deverell, a decorous and passive art historian approaching middle age, and Colin Asch, a waiflike and appealing serial killer. Written from the third-person limited-omniscient point of view, the chapters of *Soul/Mate* alternate between the perspectives of Dorothea and Colin to produce the effect that these characters do indeed mirror one another despite their differences in style. "[O]ur lives are...parallel," he asserts (119). "[T]heir predicaments were identical," she observes at a crucial point; "they were united in their desperation to escape" (196). And, in fact, Colin does serve as the agent of Dorothea's unacknowledged wishes. Standing between her and future fulfillment as the director of the prestigious Brannon Institute and the wife of her lover Charles Carpenter are two impediments—Dorothea's slanderous enemy Roger Krauss, who favors another candidate for the appointment she has been promised, and Mrs. Agnes Carpenter, Charles' alcoholic wife. By garroting Krauss and drowning Agnes, Colin clears the way for the happiness that is Dorothea's lot at the conclusion of the novel.

That Colin is Dorothea's psychological other is obvious. Where she is methodical, he is manic. Where she is self-doubting, he is narcississtic. Where she is self-abnegating, he is wildly paranoid. Where she resolutely denies, he perversely accepts. Where her personal relationships are mired in "stasis" (9), his intimate connections are resolved through deadly action.

But the otherness Colin represents has a social dimension as well. Whereas Dorothea is preternaturally sensitive to the nuances and codes of her group, Colin's self-absorption radically distorts his ability to decipher even rudimentary gestures. This is dramatically demonstrated in the first of the murders the book details:

[D]riving out of Fort Lauderdale in the red '87 Mustang with the sliding sun roof the woman had given him, which she surely wouldn't call the police to get returned . . . he happened to see, one lane over to the right, one car length ahead, a car he thought at first to be identical with his, lipstick-red, two-door coupe . . . but it turned out to be a Toyota of about that year, and what drew his attention to it like a magnet was it had a sliding sun roof too *and the roof was partway open and there was a hand stuck through it wriggling the fingers to taunt him.*
    Or was it a signal? (25)

Cornering the driver in a rest-stop men's room, Colin demands to know the meaning of the taunting wave. Explaining that he was stretching to try to keep awake, the man insists that Colin has "misread" him. Colin, however, stubbornly adhering to his own deadly misinterpretation, accuses the unfortunate motorist of having tendered a "false signal" and kills him for the crime of deceptive semantics.

    A novel, of course, is made meaningful insofar as it may be read with regard to the codes and systems it invokes. But recognizable patterns of language and culture are consistently obliterated in Colin's perversions of communication and understanding. It is pertinent that Colin is presented as the anti-author of a kind of parody of the novel. In the "Blue Ledger" Colin sets down aphoristic interpretations of his own experiences, the initials of his victims and the money he has received from them, and the coded notation of their deaths. Significantly, the codes employed involve reversal. The moment of Agnes Carpeter's murder, for example, is recorded with her initials inverted as *C.A.88104am* (182), and in the denouement of *Soul/Mate*, another meaningful reversal occurs to symbolically contradict the communicative function of the text: instead of preserving his journal, before his suicide, Colin carefully feeds it page by page into the fire.

    The transgressive other represents, then, a dislocation of basic patterns of meaning. In his "Blue Ledger" Colin carefully records Blakean comments that outline the collapse of organizational categories:

Thus "praise" and "blame" are equally unmerited.
Thus "he" (agent) and "it" (action) are falsely separated.
Thus even the most general time demarcations—"past," "present," "future"— are invalid.
For in the Blue Room (which at certain times Colin Asch was privileged to enter [through the act of murder]) all things become one. The fierce blue light erases all shadow. There is no gravity, no weight. Not even "up" and "down." (37–38)

The dissolution of contradictories characteristic of Colin's "Blue Room" makes it another version of the metaphoric zone I have defined as the "simultaneous universe" of Oates' *feminist unconscious* that precedes the social and linguistic oppositions that organize cultural meanings. At once "angel boy" and "devil twin," Colin is the intermediary between two universes of meaning—that of social repression but semantic order and that of political opportunity but incoherence. As this study argues, the very oppositions that make meaning possible—the arrangements of civilization—make it destructive or impossible in the social or family experience of many of Oates' characters. Oates' works of the "transgressive other" are, therefore, limit texts that set the theory of the feminist unconscious against the confines of family "consciousness."

The domestic investment of this confrontation is revealed in Colin's tragic history, the nature of his attraction to Dorothea, and the conclusion of the novel. For the motivation of Colin's deviance is the dramatic loss of his parents in an automobile accident in which they were both drowned:

The boy managed to get out and swim to the surface, but his father and mother were trapped inside the car, in only about eight feet of water, so the boy tried to save them, diving back down trying to get the doors of the car open, trying to pull his mother free, and then his father. . . . [A]nd it was said that Colin had gone mad in those minutes, that his mind simply shattered. (16)

Colin's subsequent actions are attempts to resolve his complex reactions to the loss of his family. His rage at his mother's abandonment finds expression in his brutal treatment of women. Significantly, he fantasizes about drowning Hartley, one of his lovers, in shallow water, and he does dispatch Agnes in this fashion. His equally powerful love for his lost mother is expressed through his adoring fixation on Dorothea, whom as Hartley reminds him "looks old enough almost to be your mother" (92). Colin chooses to murder Agnes Carpenter rather than Charles Carpenter, his rival for Dorothea's affections, because he imagines Dorothea and Charles can replace his lost parents: "It would be the most natural thing in the world; older childless couples often take up younger unattached men. A kind of spiritual adoption. 'You will never be lonely again' " (173–174). And when Colin finally kidnaps her, even obtuse Dorothea is aware that together they seem to be enacting "a grotesque parody of domesticity" (200). The conclusion of the novel finds Dorothea and Charles together about to embark on their marriage in a new house. This most uncharacteristically unambiguous ending sets the recovery of familial arrangement against the disorder Colin has introduced.

Similar domestic resolutions counter the appeal of disorder in both *American Appetites* and *Because It Is Bitter, and Because It Is My Heart*. In the first novel, a staid middle-aged man accidentally, but with much provocation and passion, kills his wife during a vituperative and drunken argument. The book is structured around the complicated issue of his guilt, and during the course of his attenuated trial, the defendant himself experiences the emotional state of otherness. "It seems so easy, somehow," Ian McCullough musingly remarks to his lawyer. "Crossing over.... To what's on the other side" (191). When the scandal first hit the newspapers, the lawyer suggested that Ian move into the Sheraton Inn under a false identity to avoid publicity. During this interval, Ian experiences an alternative self, the "Jonathan Hamilton" who signed the guest register. He wears a "pair of plastic clip-on lenses, dark green" to "give substance to his incognito" (206). He makes minor adjustments to his appearance and discovers in his assumed alter ego interests and attitudes he had not previously acknowledged in himself. But this dark liberation, which is the substance of the plot, is countered by the ironic frame of the novel. *American Appetites* commences, as does *Soul/Mate*, with the domestic ceremony of an elaborate dinner party. It concludes with another dinner party. The only substantial change is the woman who officiates.

In *Because It Is Bitter, and Because It Is My Heart*, young Iris Courtney moves from the failed family of her working-class background into an upper-class family of inherited wealth and academic stature at the conclusion. But despite the domesticity seemingly endorsed at the end of the novel, the plot concerns her experience of otherness. In an uncharacteristic gesture of chivalric bravado, a young black boy accidentally murders the retarded and repulsive Red Garlock who has been sexually menacing Iris. His differing race and his antisocial crime situate Jinx Fairchild as a fascinating "transgressive other," a "soul-mate" with whom Iris is obsessed throughout her life.

Different in plots and even in the class levels of social experience addressed, these three recent works are similar in their presentation of equivocally appealing otherness that violently controverts social standards, and in their attempts to contain that appeal within a recuperated domesticity asserted in the endings of the novels. These works of the transgressive other oscillate between the advantages and disadvantages of dual alternatives: the Utopia of Oatesian revolution confronts the bounds of Oatesian ideology. Oates' dialectics with the text underscore the complexity of both her concept of family and her practice of resistance.

THE DYNAMIC OF RESISTANCE:
OATES' LITERARY ACCOMPLISHMENT

The family in Oates' work is more than an aggregate of blood-related individuals: it is the psychosocial engine of economic power, and its gendered relationships encode that power and regulate its experiential effects. Oates' resistance to "family" defined in this way is, then, necessarily complex. According to Fredric Jameson, the romance, a form Oates has been considering and rejecting throughout her career, capitulates to false resolution, but a "literary text . . . will keep faith with impossibility . . . and insist to the end on everything problematical . . . that makes for genuine historical change" (*The Political Unconscious* 277). The value of Joyce Carol Oates' fiction does not finally rest in any solution to the problem of family in America. Instead of romances about appropriate adaptations—the good mothers and strong daughters so missed by her early critics, for example—Oates contributes to the cause of feminist revolution a genuine literature that extensively exposes the abusive definitions of power expressed through family gender restrictions in all their problematic complication.

We may outline the specifics of that contribution as follows:

1. The presentation of a gigantic "braille" of the emotions that brings to light the operation of gender ideology as it is experienced in the contemporary family.

In *Thomas Hardy and Women: Sexual Ideology and Narrative Form*, Penny Broumelha states that the function of ideology "is to offer a false resolution of real social contradictions by repressing the questions that challenge its limits and transposing, displacing, or eliding the felt contradictions of lived experience in a way that will permit of an apparent resolution" (5). The family in Oates' fiction is the locus of ideology so understood. Its distribution of the effects of power through the systematic imposition of its oppositions and negations along the lines of gender offers a false resolution of a misunderstood social predicament. Literature is, of course, also a form of ideological production, but it does not merely reflect ideology, "rather," according to Broumelha, "it produces, re-produces and transforms elements of ideology into its own literary effects" (6). Oates' domestic fiction does not, then, render the effects of gender ideology external to itself, or fully "visible"; what her literary treatment does instead is to express rather than repress the questions that challenge its limits. Oates' *oeuvre* enlarges and exploits, instead of evading, the "felt contradictions of lived experience" through the extreme sentiments of her characters. Thus, the real social contradiction between power and love is transformed by narrative into an apprehensible grid of uncomfortable relationships—mother-daughter, brother-sister, father-son, mother-son, father-daughter. Oates' closely related second accomplishment is

2.   The expression of definitions of power operating in contemporary society as narrative acts and relationships.

Since, as Terry Eagleton describes it, ideology is concerned with the "power structure and power relationships" of society (14), Oates' exhaustive narrative analysis of the American family as a structure that regulates power through gender roles and her elaborate interrogation of that structure through narratives of dyadic confrontation is an important contribution to feminist-materialist studies of "the structures of domination" (Rice-Sayer 296). But more important than Oates' articulation of power is her third feminist accomplishment:

3.   The challenge of paradigms of power: Oates' models of revolution.

Oates' fiction and her critical writing offer an alternative to the masculinist paradigm of society organized according to the deadly and exploitative competitive "I" by anticipating a shift to the cooperative "we" of the future family. In addition, the repetitious pattern of many instances of transgression and refusal promotes a form of revolution defined by Michel Foucault. It is a mistake, he argues, to think of power only in its ultimate and sovereign forms:

It seems to me that power must be understood in the first instance as the multiplicity of force relations immanent in the sphere in which they operate and which constitute their own organization; as the process which, through ceaseless struggles and confrontations, transforms, strengthens, or reverses them; as the support which these relations find in one another, thus forming a chain or system. (*The History of Sexuality,* vol. I, 92)

This concept of a "moving substrate of force relations . . . produced from one moment to the next" (93) contradicts any simple notion of a "single locus of great Refusal," according to Foucault. There is

no soul of revolt, source of all rebellions. . . . Instead there is a plurality of resistances, each of them a special case: resistances that are possible, necessary and improbable; others that are spontaneous, savage, solitary, concerted, rampant, or violent; still others that are quick to compromise, interested, or sacrificial. (96)

Oates' interrelated texts form a network of nodal struggles out of multiple resistances. Her diverse narratives of refusal and transgression comprise a dynamic revolutionary "system."

"[I]t is the strategic codification of . . . points of resistance," Foucault explains, "that makes a revolution possible" (96). Oates' extensive *oeuvre* codifies the points of resistance in a possible revolution. And her last accomplishment,

4.   The enunciation of a feminist unconcious,

opens a narrative space, reiterated through its narrative agent, the transgressive other to the text of family, that may allow the imagination of that necessary revolution in all its imperative and troubling possiblity.

Notes

INTRODUCTION

1. See Sullivan 86, Bower 34–35, and Waller's *Dreaming America*.

2. Power is, of course, a broad term. My use of it is based on Rollo May's concept in *Power and Innocence* of power as a broad continuum of "phases" and "kinds" describing an individual's ability to manipulate the environment and other people to satisfy his or her needs (41–45, 105–112). As such, *power* is a dynamic and intermediate condition derived from the authority of the state and its economic and social institutions, an interpretation shaped by class and gender.

3. See "(Woman) Writer," in which Oates advances an argument for the universality of the writer's perspective. But this highly qualified statement should be read in conjunction with "At Least I Have Made A Woman of Her: Images of Women in Yeats, Lawrence, Faulkner" that articulates strong feminist sympathies.

4. Mary Lou Parrott surveys critics who view Oates as anti-feminist; this group includes Susan Cornillon, Joanne Creighton, Marion Engle, Mary K. Grant, and Cynthia Stevens. She classifies Mary Allen, Martha Duffy, Charlotte Goodman, Linda Wagner, and Charles Markmann as critics who find Oates only moderately feminist (3–4).

5. From Franz Muller-Lyer, *The Family*, trans. F. W. Stella Browne (New York: Knopf, 1931). Quoted by Horkheimer 101–102.

6. The unspaced ellipsis (...) indicates Oates' omissions. I use the spaced ellipsis (. . .) to indicate my own omissions.

7. My use of the term assumes Louis Althusser's definition: "What is represented in ideology is not the system of real relations which govern the existence of individuals, but the imaginary relation of those individuals to the real relations in which they live" (165).

8. For the source material for the following explanation of Jameson's use of the semiotic rectangle, see Greimas and Rastier's original article (86–105) and Jameson, *The Political Unconscious* 47–49, 166–169, 242–280.

CHAPTER 1

1. According to Friedman, "Herz is the fierce, Old Testament God who orders his faithful and devoted daughter Karen (Abraham) to kill Shar (Isaac), the only man she has found worthy of her love" (23).
2. See Waller 99–100 and Creighton, *Joyce Carol Oates* for discussions of D. H. Lawrence's influence on *With Shuddering Fall.*

CHAPTER 2

1. According to Paula J. Caplan, who surveyed the marked tendency to fault mothers in psychological studies, mother blaming is detrimental to society because it prevents us from seeing the "total range of causes for children's unhappiness and psychological problems" (70).
2. See Gregory Bateson, *Steps to an Ecology of Mind;* Ann Dally, *Inventing Motherhood* 230–235; and Kathy Wexler, *Family Therapy* (6).
3. My use of the theory of the schizophrenogenic mother is not to argue for its accuracy. This, like all of the psychological theories I make use of, I am assuming are cultural accounts available to Oates that she makes use of, not to prove them but to question the culture in which they are implicated.
4. Dr. Tantram tells Karen Herz when she is about to leave the mental hospital that, unlike most of his patients, who are "imprisoned, waiting to die," she is "self-cured" through the force of her own "will" (*With Shuddering Fall* 209).
5. McNall's argument derives from preoedipal object relations theory and Carl Jung's concept of integration:

our first mental representations of the mother are of a "good object" and a "bad object," the being who is there taking proper care of our needs, and the one who is absent or rejecting or stifling. To these images . . . are attached two conflicting mental representations of self. . . . The main developmental task is to integrate the two sets of images. (6)

6. See also "Year of Wonders" in *The Seduction and Other Stories* for a more positive presentation of the motif of pictures as an expression of mother-daughter issues of similarity-dissimilarity and connection-individuation.
7. In *Joyce Carol Oates*, Ellen G. Friedman discusses Oates' continuing fascination with the *Alice* books as a basis for her interpretation of *Wonderland* (95–98). *The Profane Art* contains Oates' essay on "Charles Dodgson's Golden Hours." In both "Other Celebrity Voices" and "Stories That Define Me: The

Making of a Writer" Oates acknowledges the early and profound influence of the Carroll books.

8. Although Oates claims in her "Author's Note" to *them* that "the 'Maureen Wendall' of this narrative" was actually a student in a night course who wrote a few years later and gradually unfolded her story (5), Sanford Pinsker points out in "The Blue Collar Apocalypse, or Detroit Bridge's Falling Down: Joyce Carol Oates' *them*" that the character was "a composite drawn from several students" ("Speaking about Short Fiction" 35).

9. As Oates explained to Linda Kuehl, "This is something that happened to me too, and both of us responded in a very weak, rather victimized way, by being annihilated almost and reduced to tears and despair by a foolish event" ("An Interview with Joyce Carol Oates" 5).

10. The "disease" of women's sexuality, from birth defects to female disorders, a constant topic of the women who surround Maureen, is especially apparent in the vehement warnings of Carol's mother:

about how girls should never go into cellars or dark places, never sit on toilet seats in public places, or look at men in the street, or hang around anywhere, or wash their hair during that time of the month—or else they would get very sick and everyone would know why—and did they know how easy it was to get pregnant and have a baby? (150)

11. According to Cleanth Brooks, R. W. B. Lewis, and Robert Penn Warren, "Whitman seems to be telling us most indirectly how he as an individual man . . . became a poet, and a poet who, as in Emerson's definition, eventually takes to himself the attributes and functions of the outmoded divinities" (933).

12. Quoted in Thrale, Hibbard, and Holman (432).

13. It is somewhat unfair to cite Howells as the spokesman for puritanical restriction, because he argues that a "tradition of decency" flourishes because it is "on the whole . . . truer to life" (448).

CHAPTER 3

1. Propp researched the Russian tale, but his morphology has general application to much folklore. The elements of the tale are outlined in his Chapter III, 25–70.

2. See James R. Giles, "From Jimmy Gatz to Jules Wendall," for a discussion of the influence of *The Great Gatsby* on *them*.

3. For G. F. Waller, Jules demonstrates the transcendence of hope, "a buoyant romantic affirmation" (135–142), whereas for Ellen Friedman Jules represents the antiromantic acceptance of limits (73–93). Joanne Creighton's Jules triumphs over naturalistic determination (*Joyce Carol Oates* 63–93), whereas Mary Kathryn Grant's Jules is ultimately a figure of tragic impotence (133–134).

4. See especially Chapters I–III.

5. The dedication of the novel to Robert Fagles, translator of *The Oresteia*, "in honor of his service in the House of Atreus" substantiates this correlation.

6. This epithet appears in the concluding argument of "A Plea for Captain John Brown" (Thoreau).

7. In *The New York Times Book Review* of March 29, 1981, during the same year *Angel of Light* was published, Oates replied to the omnipresent inquiry, "Why Is Your Writing So Violent?" in an article of that title. Citing the tradition of twentieth-century realism and the "bias" of "proper" subjects for women, Oates described critical concern about the violence of her work as "always insulting," "always ignorant," and "always sexist" (15).

8. Oates' analyses of Yeats' use of tragic forms appearing in *The Edge of Impossibility* enlarge on the ritual of violent sympathy Nick describes. "Character is present only in comedy; in tragedy its place is taken by passions, motives, and events, and moments of ritualistic violence and beauty" (141). The purpose of these moments, Oates explains, is not "thematic": in Yeats' works, "dramatizations are clearly meant to subject the viewer to a certain violent rearrangement of his experience as viewer, along with the more crucial rearrangement of his experience as a human being" (146). One powerful effect of this rearrangement through violent spectacle is in Yeats' words, "a drowning and breaking of the dykes that separate man from man" (150).

9. The opposing principles Oates assigns to Nick and Maurie are prefigured by the antithesis Oates uncovers in Dostoevski's *The Brothers Karamazov*. "The existentialist [Nick] accepts all responsibility for his actions . . . but accepts no responsibility for actions that are not his own," whereas the "essentialist (in this context the ideal Christian) [Maurie] accepts all guilt for all actions" and has "no singular identity," but his failing is that "ultimately" he "has no responsibility" at all (*"Tragic and Comic Vision in The Brothers Karamazov"* 96).

10. Beside the parallels suggested by Nick's name, personality, and actions, the second portion of Oates' dedication—"for our lost generations"—introduces a link with Hemingway.

CHAPTER 4

1. In *Death in Life: Survivors of Hiroshima*, Robert Jay Lifton fully describes the characteristic psychic numbness and survivor guilt that Jesse experiences in the aftermath of the murders.

2. Jameson cites *Tristes tropiques* 199. A key point in his theory of literature as representing a "political unconscious," this earlier explanation (383–385) is elaborated in *The Political Unconscious* 77ff.

3. Explaining to Dale Boesky that she had "deliberately forced the ending" of *Wonderland*, Oates confided: "I kept thinking about it, and . . . had to go back and write the true ending. . . . When I say *had to* I am not exaggerating, I felt that I had unleashed a kind of perverted, misrepresentative horror upon the world" ("Correspondence with Miss Joyce Carol Oates" 476).

4. In *Power and Innocence*, May defines *exploitative power* as total control of others. Identified with force, it "always presupposes violence or the threat of violence" toward victims who are allowed "no choice or spontaneity" (105–106). *Nutrient power* is cooperative and supportive "power *for* the other" (109). I identify this kind of power with Winnicott's "good-enough" parental care discussed in Chapter 2.

CHAPTER 5

1. In her Introduction to *The Female Body in Western Culture*, Susan Robin Suleiman, states: "The cultural significance of the female body is . . . that of a *symbolic construct*. Everything we know about the body . . . exists for us in some form of discourse" (2).

2. When Linda Kuehl asked if Swan was a participant in "a Freudian triangle," Oates replied:

Domestic romance? Yes, *A Garden of Earthly Delights* does have that, though it's not really a triangle. It's more between the boy and his mother. Strictly speaking, to have this Freudian romance, one must have a good strong father figure, so it's not quite that...but close to it, I think. ("An Interview with Joyce Carol Oates" 308)

3. M. Charles Albert Cingria is cited by de Rougemont as the author of this passage.

4. Nancy Chodorow observes that: "Unfortunately (from the point of view of the naively egotistic infant) its mother has (and always has had) things to do which take her away from it" (68–69).

CHAPTER 6

1. See "The Psychogenesis of a Case of Female Homosexuality" and "Some Psychical Consequences of the Anatomical Distinction between the Sexes."

2. See *Quarterly Review of Literature* 15 (1968): 393–409.

3. The term is introduced by the child's grandmother (172).

4. See "The Dissolution of the Oedipus Complex" (178–179) and "Some Psychical Consequences of the Anatomical Distinction between the Sexes" (252–256).

5. Chodorow quotes Janine Chasseguet-Smirgel, "Feminine guilt and the Oedipus Complex," *Female Sexuality* (Ann Arbor: University of Michigan Press, 1970), 118.

CHAPTER 7

1. This episode also appears in "The Going Away Party," the short story Oates has chosen to represent her own work in the anthology *Story* that she coedited in 1985 (807–820).

2. Oates also treats the theme of the international conference in the "Our Wall" section of stories collected in *Last Days*.

3. Thomas Traherne's poem "Shadows in the Water," similar in imagery to Hiram's vision, also contains an answer to his question:

> . . . .
> Thus did I by the water's brink
> Another world beneath me think;
> And while the lofty spacious skies
> Reversed there, abused mine eyes,
> I fancied other feet
> Came mine to touch or meet;
>
> . . . .
> O ye that stand upon the brink,
> Whom I so near me through the chink
> With wonder see: what faces there,
> Whose feet, whose bodies do ye wear?
> I my companions see
> In you, another me.
> They seem others, but are we;
> Our second selves these shadows be.

4. In the Preface to *Where Are You Going, Where Have You Been?: Stories of Young America* (1974), Oates proclaimed: "A new morality is emerging in North America . . . the democratization of the spirit, the experiencing of life as meaningful in itself, without divisions into 'good' or 'bad,' 'beautiful' or 'ugly,' 'moral' or 'immoral' " (9).

References

Abel, Elizabeth. *Writing and Sexual Difference*. Chicago: University of Chicago Press, 1982.

Allen, Mary Inez. "The Terrified Women of Joyce Carol Oates." *The Necessary Blankness: Women in Major American Fiction of the Sixties*. Urbana: University of Illinois Press, 1976. 133–154.

Althusser, Louis. "Ideology and Ideological State Apparatuses." *Lenin and Philosophy and Other Essays*. Trans. Ben Brewster. New York: Monthly Review Press, 1971.

Bateson, Gregory. *Steps to an Ecology of Mind*. London: Paladin, 1973.

Beckson, Karl, and Arthur Ganz. *A Reader's Guide to Literary Terms*. New York: Farrar, 1960.

Belsey, Catherine. *Critical Practice*. New York: Methuen, 1980.

Bettelheim, Bruno. *The Uses of Enchantment: The Meaning and Importance of Fairy Tales*. New York: Knopf, 1977.

Bower, Warren. "Bliss in the First Person." *Saturday Review* 26 Oct. 1968: 34–35.

Brooks, Cleanth, R.W.B. Lewis, and Robert Penn Warren. "Walt Whitman." *American Literature: The Makers and the Making*. 4 vols. New York: St. Martin's, 1974. Vol. B.

Broumelha, Penny. *Thomas Hardy and Women: Sexual Ideology and Narrative Form*. Totowa, NJ: Barnes, 1982.

Caplan, Paula J. "Take the Blame Off Mother." *Psychology Today* Oct. 1982: 70–71.

Chesler, Phyllis. *Women and Madness*. 1972. New York: Avon, 1973.

Chodorow, Nancy. *The Reproduction of Mothering: Psychoanalysis and the Sociology of Gender*. Los Angeles: University of California Press, 1978.

Creighton, Joanne V. *Joyce Carol Oates*. Twayne's United States Authors Series 321. Boston: Twayne, 1979.

_____ . "Unliberated Women in Joyce Carol Oates's Fiction." *Critical Essays on Joyce Carol Oates*. Ed. Linda W. Wagner. Boston: G. K. Hall, 1979. 149–156.

Culler, Jonathan. *On Deconstruction: Theory and Criticism after Structuralism*. Ithaca, N.Y.: Cornell University Press, 1982.

Dally, Ann. *Inventing Motherhood*. New York: Schocken, 1982.

Dalton, Elizabeth. "Joyce Carol Oates: Violence in the Head." *Commentary* June 1970: 75–77.

Daly, Brenda O. "Narrator Hermaphrodite: Voices in the Visionary Art of Joyce Carol Oates." Diss. University of Minnesota, 1985.

de Rougemont, Denis. *Love in the Western World*. 1940. Trans. Montgomery Belgion. New York: Pantheon, 1956.

Donovan, Josephine. Ed. *Feminist Literary Criticism: Explanations in Theory*. Lexington: University of Kentucky Press, 1989.

Dowling, William C. *Jameson, Althusser, and Marx: An Introduction to "The Political Unconscious."* Ithaca, NY: Cornell University Press, 1984.

Eagleton, Terry. *Literary Theory: An Introduction*. Minneapolis: University of Minnesota Press, 1983.

Fiedler, Leslie A. "Come Back to the Raft Ag'in, Huck Honey!" *An End to Innocence: Essays and Culture*. New York: Stein and Day, 1972.

Fossum, Robert H. "Only Control: The Novels of Joyce Carol Oates." *Critical Essays on Joyce Carol Oates*. Ed. Linda W. Wagner. Boston: G. K. Hall, 1979. 49–60.

Foucault, Michel. *The History of Sexuality*. 3 vols. Trans. Robert Hurley. New York: Pantheon, 1978. Vol. I.

_____ . "Preface to Transgression." *Language, Counter-Meaning, Practice: Selected Essays and Interviews*. Ed. and trans. Donald F. Bouchard, trans. Sherry Simon. Ithaca, NY: Cornell University Press, 1977.

Freud, Sigmund. *The Standard Edition of the Complete Works of Sigmund Freud*. 24 vols. Ed. and trans. James Strachey. London: The Hogarth Press, 1961.

_____ . "The Dissolution of the Oedipus Complex." *Standard Edition*. Vol. XIX.

_____ . "Letter to Fliess, no. 71, 15 Oct. 1897." *Standard Edition*. Vol. I.

_____ . "The Resistance to Psycho-Analysis." *Standard Edition*. Vol. XIX.

_____ . "Some Psychical Consequences of the Anatomical Distinction between the Sexes." *Standard Edition*. Vol. XIX.

_____ . "The Psychogenesis of a Case of Female Homosexuality." *Standard Edition*. Vol. XVIII.

Friedman, Ellen G. *Joyce Carol Oates*. New York: Ungar, 1980.

Friedrich, Otto. *Going Crazy: An Inquiry into the Madness of Our Time*. New York: Avon, 1977.

Frye, Northrop. *Anatomy of Criticism: Four Essays*. Princeton, NJ: Princeton University Press, 1957.

Frye, Northrop, Sheridan Baker, and George Perkins. *The Harper Handbook to Literature*. New York: Harper, 1985.

Giles, James R. "From Jimmy Gatz to Jules Wendall." *Dalhousie* 56 (1976–1977): 718–724.

Gordon, Mary. "The Life and Hard Times of Cinderella." Rev. of *Marya*, by Joyce Carol Oates. *New York Times Book Review* 2 Mar. 1986: 7ff.

Grant, Mary Kathryn. *The Tragic Vision of Joyce Carol Oates*. Durham, NC: Duke University Press, 1978.

"The Great Goddess." *Larousse Encyclopedia of Mythology*. London: Paul Hamlyn, 1959. 86–89.

Greene, Gayle and Coppélia Kahn. Eds. *Making a Difference: Feminist Literary Criticism*. New York: Methuen, 1985.

Greimas, A. J., and F. Rastier. "The Interaction of Semiotic Constraints." *Game, Play, Literature*. 1968. Ed. Jacques Ehrmann. Yale French Studies. Boston: Beacon, 1971.

Guntrip, Harry. *Psychoanalytical Theory, Therapy and the Self*. New York: Basic, 1971.

Hassan, Ihab. *Radical Innocence: The Contemporary American Novel*. Princeton, NJ: Princeton University Press, 1961.

Hawthorne, Nathaniel. *The House of the Seven Gables*. New York: Books, Inc., n.d.

Henkins, Katharine Maine. "Joyce Carol Oates's America." Diss. Claremont Graduate School, 1986.

Horkheimer, Max. "Authority and the Family." *Critical Theory*. Trans. Matthew J. O'Connell and others. New York: Continuum, 1982.

Howells, William Dean. *Criticism and Fiction*. Excerpted in *The American Tradition in Literature*. 5th ed. 2 vols. Ed. Sculley Bradley et al. New York: Random, 1981. Vol. 1.

Jameson, Fredric. "Cognitive Mapping." *Marxism and the Interpretation of Culture*. Ed. Cary Nelson and Lawrence Grossberg. Urbana: University of Illinois Press, 1988. 347–357.

_____. *Marxism and Form: Twentieth-Century Dialectical Theories of Literature*. Princeton, NJ: Princeton University Press, 1971.

_____. *The Political Unconscious: Narrative as a Socially Symbolic Act*. Ithaca, NY: Cornell University Press, 1981.

Jones, Ernest. *The Life and Work of Sigmund Freud*. 3 vols. New York: Basic, 1957.

Kristeva, Julia. "Stabat Mater." *The Female Body in Western Culture*. Ed. Susan Rubin Suleiman. Cambridge, MA: Harvard University Press, 1986.

Lacan, Jacques. "The Meaning of the Phallus." *Feminine Sexuality: Jacques Lacan and the* "école freudienne." Ed. Juliet Mitchell and Jacqueline Rose. Trans. Jacqueline Rose. New York: Norton, 1985. 74–85.

Lasch, Christopher. *Haven in a Heartless World: The Family Besieged.* New York: Basic, 1957.

Lercangee, Francine. *Joyce Carol Oates: An Annotated Bibliography.* With Preface and annotations by Bruce F. Michelson. New York: Garland, 1986.

Levi-Strauss, Claude. *Elementary Structures of Kinship.* Trans. James Haile Bell, John Richard von Sturmer, and Rodney Needham. Boston: Beacon, 1969.

————. "Reciprocity, the Essence of Social Life." *The Family: Its Structures and Functions.* Ed. Rose Laub Cosner. New York: St. Martin's, 1974. 3–12.

Lewis, C. S. *The Allegory of Love: A Study in Medieval Tradition.* New York: Oxford University Press, 1958.

Lewis, R.W.B. *The American Adam: Innocence, Tragedy, and Tradition in the Nineteenth Century.* Chicago: University of Chicago Press, 1958.

Lifton, Robert Jay. *Death in Life: Survivors of Hiroshima.* New York: Simon and Schuster, 1967.

Maney, Margaret Shaeffer. "The Urban Apocalypse in Contemporary Novels." *DAI* 42 (1980): 2,111A. University of Miami.

May, Rollo. *Power and Innocence: A Search for the Sources of Violence.* New York: Norton, 1972.

McNall, Sally Allen. *Who Is in the House?: A Psychological Study of Two Centuries of Women's Fiction in America, 1795 to the Present.* New York: Elsevier, 1981.

Mickelson, Anne Z. "Sexual Love in the Fiction of Joyce Carol Oates." *Reaching Out: Sensitivity and Order in Recent American Fiction by Women.* Metuchen, NJ: Scarecrow Press, 1979. 15–34.

Milazzo, Lee, ed. *Conversations with Joyce Carol Oates.* Jackson: University of Mississippi Press, 1989.

Miller, Michael Vincent. Rev. of *Forbidden Partners: The Incest Taboo in Modern Culture.* By James B. Twitchell. *New York Times Book Review* 18 Jan. 1987: 7–8.

Mitchell, Juliet. *Feminine Sexuality: Jacques Lacan and the "école freudienne."* Ed. Juliet Mitchell and Jacqueline Rose. New York: Norton, 1985.

————. *Psychoanalysis and Feminism: Freud, Reich, Laing and Women.* New York: Vintage, 1971.

Newton, Judith, and Deborah Rosenfelt, Eds. *Femininst Criticism and Social Change: Sex, Class and Race in Literature and Culure.* London: Methuen, 1985.

Newton, Judith L., Mary P. Ryan, and Judith R. Walkowitz, Eds. *Sex and Class in Women's History.* Boston: Routledge & Kegan Paul, 1983.

Norman, Torborg. *Isolation and Contact: A Study of Character Relationships in Joyce Carol Oates's Short Stories 1963–1980.* Goteborg, Swed.: *Acta Universitatis Gothoburgenis,* 1984.

Oates, Joyce Carol. *American Appetites.* New York: Dutton, 1989.

_____ . *Angel of Light*. New York: Dutton, 1981.

_____ . *The Assassins: A Book of Hours*. 1975. Greenwich: Fawcett, 1983.

_____ . "At Least I Have Made a Woman of Her: Images of Women in Yeats, Lawrence, Faulkner." *The Profane Art*. 35–62.

_____ . *Because It Is Bitter, and Because It Is My Heart*. New York: Dutton, 1990.

_____ . *Bellefleur*. New York: Warner, 1980.

_____ . *By the North Gate*. New York: Vanguard, 1963.

_____ . "Charles Dodgson's Golden Hours." *The Profane Art*. 82–89.

_____ . "Childhood." *Epoch* 16. (iii) (Spring 1967): 204–222.

_____ . *Childwold*. New York: Fawcett, 1976.

_____ . *Contraries: Essays*. New York: Oxford University Press, 1981.

_____ . "Correspondence with Miss Joyce Carol Oates." With Dale Boesky. *International Review of Psychoanalysis* 2 (1975): 481–486.

_____ . *Crossing the Border: Fifteen Tales*. New York: Vanguard, 1976.

_____ . *Cybele*. Santa Barbara: Black Sparrow, 1979.

_____ . "The Dark Lady of American Letters: An Interview with Joyce Carol Oates." With Joe David Bellamy. *The New Fiction: Interviews with Innovative American Writers*. Urbana: University of Illinois Press, 1974. 19–31.

_____ . "The Death Throes of Romanticism: The Poetry of Sylvia Plath." *New Heaven, New Earth*. 111–114.

_____ . *Do with Me What You Will*. 1973. New York: Fawcett, 1983.

_____ . *The Edge of Impossibility: Tragic Forms in Literature*. 1972. Greenwich: Fawcett, 1973.

_____ . *Expensive People*. Greenwich: Fawcett, 1968.

_____ . *A Garden of Earthly Delights*. 1967. Greenwich: Fawcett, 1969.

_____ . *The Goddess and Other Women*. New York: Fawcett, 1974.

_____ . "The Going Away Party." *Story: Fictions Past and Present*. Ed. Boyd Litzinger and Joyce Carol Oates. New York: Heath, 1985. 807–820.

_____ . "The Hostile Sun: The Poetry of D. H. Lawrence." *New Heaven, New Earth*. 37–83.

_____ . "Imaginary Cities: America." *The Profane Art*. 9–34.

_____ . "An Interview with Joyce Carol Oates." With Linda Kuehl. *Commonweal* 5 Dec. 1969: 307–310.

_____ . "Joyce Carol Oates on Harriette Arnow's *The Dollmaker*." *The Dollmaker*. By Harriette Arnow. 1954. New York: Avon, 1972. 601–608.

_____ . "Kafka's Paradise." *New Heaven, New Earth*. 247–276.

_____ . *Last Days: Stories*. New York: Dutton, 1984.

_____ . "Legendary Jung." *The Profane Art*. 159–164.

_____ . "The Magnanimity of *Wuthering Heights*." *The Profane Art*. 63–81.

_____ . *Marriages and Infidelities: Short Stories*. New York: Fawcett, 1972.

_____ . *Marya: A Life*. New York: Dutton, 1986.

_____ . "The Molesters." *Quarterly Review of Literature* 15 (1968) 393–409.

_____. Afterword. *Mysteries of Winterthurn.* 1984. New York: Berkley, 1985. 514–516.

_____. "The Myth of the Isolated Artist." *Psychology Today* May 1983: 74–75.

_____. *New Heaven, New Earth: The Visionary Experience in Literature.* New York: Vanguard, 1974.

_____. *Night-Side: Eighteen Tales.* New York: Vanguard, 1977.

_____. *On Boxing.* New York: Doubleday, 1987.

_____. "Other Celebrity Voices: How Art Has Touched Our Lives." *Today's Health* May 1974: 31.

_____. *The Profane Art: Essays and Reviews.* New York: Dutton, 1983.

_____. "Pseudonymous Selves." *(Woman) Writer.* 383–397.

_____. *The Seduction and Other Stories.* Santa Barbara: Black Sparrow, 1976.

_____. *Solstice.* New York: Dutton, 1985.

_____. *Son of the Morning.* New York: Vanguard, 1978.

_____. *Soul/Mate.* New York: Dutton, 1989.

_____. "Speaking about Short Fiction." With Sanford Pinsker. *Conversations with Joyce Carol Oates.* Ed. Milazzo. Jackson: Universtity of Mississippi Press, 1989. 95–100.

_____. "Stories That Define Me: The Making of a Writer." *New York Times Book Review* 11 July 1982: 1ff.

_____. "A Terrible Beauty Is Born. How?" *New York Times Book Review* 11 Aug. 1985: 1ff.

_____. *them.* 1969. Greenwich: Fawcett, 1970.

_____. "Tragic and Comic Visions in *The Brothers Karamazov.*" *The Edge of Impossiblity.* 78–101.

_____. "Tragic Rites in Yeats's *A Full Moon in March.*" *The Edge of Impossibility.* 146–164.

_____. "Transformations of Self: An Interview with Joyce Carol Oates." *Ohio Review* 15 (1973): 50–61.

_____. *The Triumph of the Spider Monkey.* New York: Fawcett, 1976.

_____. *Unholy Loves.* New York: Vanguard, 1979.

_____. *Upon the Sweeping Flood and Other Stories.* 1966. Greenwich: Fawcett, 1971.

_____. *The Wheel of Love and Other Stories.* 1970. Greenwich: Fawcett, 1972.

_____. "When Characters from the Page Turn to Flesh on the Screen." *New York Times* 23 Mar. 1986: B1ff.

_____. *Where Are You Going, Where Have You Been?: Stories of Young America.* Greenwich: Fawcett, 1974.

_____. "Why Is Your Writing So Violent?" *New York Times Book Review* 29 Mar. 1981: 15ff.

_____. *With Shuddering Fall.* 1964. Greenwich: Fawcett, 1971.

_____ . "(Woman) Writer." *(Woman Writer): Occasions and Opportunities.* New York: Dutton, 1988. 22–32.

_____ . *Wonderland.* 1971. Greenwich: Fawcett, 1973.

_____ . "Wonderlands." *Georgia Review* 38 (1984): 487–506.

_____ . *You Must Remember This.* New York: Dutton, 1987.

Parrott, Mary Lou. "Subversive Conformity: Feminism and Motherhood in Joyce Carol Oates." Diss. University of Maryland, 1983.

Parsons, Talcott. "Incest." *The Family: Its Structure and Functions.* Ed. Cosner. New York: St. Martin's Press, 1974. 13–30.

Propp, V. *Morphology of the Folk Tale.* 1928. Trans. Laurence Scott. Austin: University of Texas Press, 1977.

Ramas, Maria. "Freud's Dora, Dora's Hysteria." *Sex and Class in Women's History.* Ed. Newton, et al. Boston: Routledge & Kegan Paul, 1983. 72–113.

Rank, Otto. *The Myth of the Birth of the Hero.* Trans. Robbins Jelliffe. New York: Nervous and Mental Disease Monographs, 1914.

Rapp, Rayna. "Household and Family." *Sex and Class in Women's History.* Ed. Newton et al. Boston: Routledge & Kegan Paul, 1983. 233–9.

Rice-Sayer, Laura. "Domination and Desire: A Feminist-Materialist Reading of Manuel Puig's *Kiss of the Spider Woman.*" *Textual Analysis: Some Readers Reading.* Ed. Mary Ann Caws. New York: MLA, 1986.

Rourke, Constance. *American Humor: A Study of the National Character.* New York: Harcourt, 1931.

Rubin, Gayle. "The Traffic in Women: Notes on the 'Political Economy of Sex.' " *Toward an Anthropology of Women.* Ed. Rayna R. Reiter. New York: Monthly Review Press, 1975.

Santiago, Luciano P. R. *The Children of Oedipus: Brother-Sister: Incest in Psychiatry, Literature, History and Mythology.* Roslyn Heights, NY: Libra Publishers, 1973.

Selden, Raman. *A Reader's Guide to Contemporary Literary Theory.* Lexington: University Press of Kentucky.

Showalter, Elaine. "My Friend, Joyce Carol Oates: An Intimate Portrait." *Ms.* Mar. 1986: 44ff.

Silverman, Kaja. *The Subject of Semiotics.* New York: Oxford University Press, 1983.

Stevens, Cynthia Charlotte. "The Imprisoned Imagination: The Family in the Fiction of Joyce Carol Oates, 1960–1970." Diss. University of Illinois at Urbana-Champaign, 1974.

Suleiman, Susan Rubin, Ed. *The Female Body in Western Culture: Contemporary Perspectives.* Cambridge: Harvard University Press, 1986. 99–118.

Sullivan, Walter. "The Artificial Demon: Joyce Carol Oates and the Dimension of the Real." *Critical Essays on Joyce Carol Oates.* Ed. Linda W. Wagner. Boston: G. K. Hall, 1979. 77–86.

Tanner, Tony. *Adultery in the Novel: Contract and Transgression.* Baltimore: Johns Hopkins University Press, 1979.

Thoreau, Henry David. "A Plea for Captain John Brown." *Major Writers of America*. Ed. Perry Miller et. al. New York: Harcourt, 1962.

Thrale, William Flint, Addison Hibbard, and C. Hugh Holman, eds. "Pastoral." *A Handbook to Literature*. New York: Odyssey, 1960.

Traherne, Thomas. "Shadows in the Water." *Seventeenth-Century Prose and Poetry*. Ed. Alexander M. Witherspoon and Frank J. Warnke. New York: Harcourt, 1963. 1,029.

Trilling, Lionel. *The Liberal Imagination*. New York: Viking, 1950.

Waggoner, Hyatt H. *American Poets: From Puritans to the Present*. Boston: Houghton Miffin, 1978.

Wagner, Linda W., ed. *Critical Essays on Joyce Carol Oates*. Boston: G. K. Hall, 1979.

Waller, G. F. *Dreaming America: Obsession and Transcendence in the Fiction of Joyce Carol Oates*. Baton Rouge: Louisiana State University Press, 1979.

Wegs, Joyce M. " 'Don't You Know Who I Am?' The Grotesque in Oates's 'Where Are You Going, Where Have You Been?' " *Critical Essays on Joyce Carol Oates*. Ed Linda W. Wagner. Boston: G. K. Hall, 1979. 87–92.

Wexler, Kathy. *Family Therapy*. Los Angeles: The Association for Advanced Training in the Behavioral Sciences, 1983.

Whitman, Walt. "Song of Myself." *Leaves of Grass*. Ed. Harold W. Blodgett and Sculley Bradley. New York: Norton, 1968.

Winnicott, D. W. *The Maturational Process and the Facilitating Environment*. New York: International Universities Press, 1965.

Wolfe, Linda. "Psycho Killer." Rev. of *Soul/Mate*. *New York Times Book Review* 4 June 1989: 16.

Index

About the Author

MARILYN C. WESLEY is an Assistant Professor in the Department of English at Hartwick College in New York. She received her Ph.D. from Syracuse University (1988) with a concentration in American literature and literary theory and has published a number of articles in her field with particular emphasis on Joyce Carol Oates.